The History of English Handwriting

AD 700–1400

xlii·

HWÆT WE FEOR ⁊ NEA
gefrigen habbað· ofer middan geard
moyses domas· wræclico word
riht· wera cneorissum· in uprodor
eadigra gehwam· æfter bealu siðe· bote lifes·
lifigendra gehwam· lang sumne ræd· hæleðū
secgan· gehyre se ðe wille· þone on westenne·
weroda drihten· soðfæst cyning· mid his sylfes
miht gewyrðode· ⁊ him wundra fela· ece alwalda·
in æht forgeaf· he wæs leof gode· leoda aldor·
horsc ⁊ hreðer gleaw· herges wisa· freom folc
toga· faraones cyn· godes andsaca· gyrd wite
band· þær him gesealde· sigora waldend· mod
gum mago ræswum· his maga feorh· onwist eð
les· abrahames sunum· heah wæs þ hand lean·
⁊ him hold frea gesealde wæpna geweald· wið
wraðra gryre· ofercom mid þy campe· cneoma-
ga fela· feonda folc riht· ða wæs for
ma sið· þ hine weroda god· wordum nægde· þær
he him gesægde· soð wundra fela· hu þas woruld
worhte· witig drihten· eorðan ymb hwyrft· ⁊ up
rodor· gesette sigerice· ⁊ his sylfes naman·
ðone yldo bearn· ær ne cuðon· frod fædera
cyn· þeah hie fela wiston··

Fig. 1 Bodleian MS. Junius 11, late tenth century.

The History of English Handwriting

AD 700 – 1400

Sir Edward Maunde Thompson

Revised and augmented by
Gerrish Gray

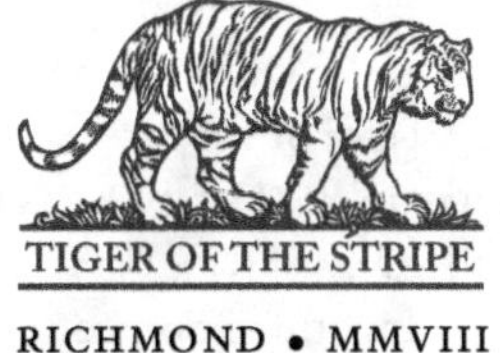

RICHMOND • MMVIII

This edition
first published in 2008 by
Tiger of the Stripe
50 Albert Road
Richmond
Surrey TW10 6DP
United Kingdom

ISBN 978 1 904799 10 8

Typeset in the United Kingdom by
Tiger of the Stripe
Printed in the United Sates and
the United Kingdom by
Lightning Source

Introduction to the Tiger of the Stripe Edition

By Gerrish Gray

Sir Edward Maunde Thompson (1840–1929) was one of the outstanding palæographers of his generation and founded the Palæographical Society in 1873. He modestly described his magisterial *Introduction to Greek and Latin Palæography*, first published in 1893 and revised in 1912, as 'a fairly complete account of the history and progress of Greek and Latin palaeography.' It is still in print today.*

After Rugby and Oxford, he entered the British Museum (now British Library) as assistant in the office of the Principal Librarian. He was made Keeper of Manuscripts in 1878 and Principal Librarian in 1888.

He delivered *The History of English Handwriting* before the Bibliographical Society in 1899 and it was published in the Society's *Transactions* in the following year. This edition is based on the offprint of that article and reproduces nearly all the original illustrations.

In addition, the number of illustrations has been increased from eighteen to forty-eight. Transcriptions have been added to eight of these, making the work a useful introduction to English paleography.

* Oxbow Books, 2002. Tiger of the Stripe is also preparing an edition.

List of Illustrations

The History of English Handwriting AD 700–1400

By Sir Edward Maunde Thompson, KCB

In this book I propose to follow the development of handwriting in England from the beginning of the eighth century to the close of the fourteenth century, paying special attention to the finer types of which specimens have survived. The history of handwriting in England is of more than ordinary interest. At the earliest period we find two rival styles competing for the lead in literary works, the one being the native hand, as I will venture to call the handwriting which was first introduced from Ireland: an adaptation of the old Roman half-uncial hand, which also played so important a part in the development of the Western writing of the Middle Ages; the other being the uncial hand which the Roman missionaries brought with them into this country and which at certain centres had some success, but which eventually disappeared before its more vigorous opponent. Then followed the growth of the national handwriting of the Anglo-Saxon period; and this in its turn gave place to the foreign minuscule writing, which first began to make its way into England when she politically came into closer contact with the Continent of Europe, and which became the accepted character of writing when the Norman conquest subjected her entirely to foreign rule and to foreign ideas. After that period the history of writing in England is a branch of the history of writing of Western Europe. The English hand of the later middle age is a development of the

Carolingian minuscule hand, cast, however, in an English mould and thus having a distinctive national character.

In the seventh century there existed in the north of England a famous school of writing, which has been named the School of Lindisfarne, from the place where it was specially fostered. In extant MSS, preserved at Durham and in the British Library, and at Oxford and Cambridge, we have a fair amount of material from which to learn the characteristics of this northern hand. In the early part of the eighth century it was already developed in two forms: as a book-hand and as a cursive hand. The Lindisfarne Gospels, or Durham Book, in the British Library, is a standard of the finest literary type; in more ordinary manuscripts and in charters we have numerous specimens of the cursive hand. This northern hand, particularly in its cursive form, was speedily adopted throughout the country and imbibed in the several kingdoms of the Heptarchy local characteristics which are in some instances marked enough to enable us to discriminate between examples from different districts.

For the origin of the northern English hand, we have to seek in Ireland; and among the earliest specimens of the writing of that country there is one which, before all others, gives the key. This is the fragmentary copy of the Gospels in Latin (MS. A. 4, 15), in the Library of Trinity College Dublin, which may be dated in the latter half of the seventh century. The resemblance between the writing of this MS (Fig. 2) and the Roman half-uncial hand is so striking that there can be no hesitation in connecting them. Both uncial and half-uncial manuscripts must have found their way into Ireland in the hands of missionaries from Rome and other places abroad; but, judging from the extant remains of early Irish writing, it is quite evident that the half-uncial hand alone obtained

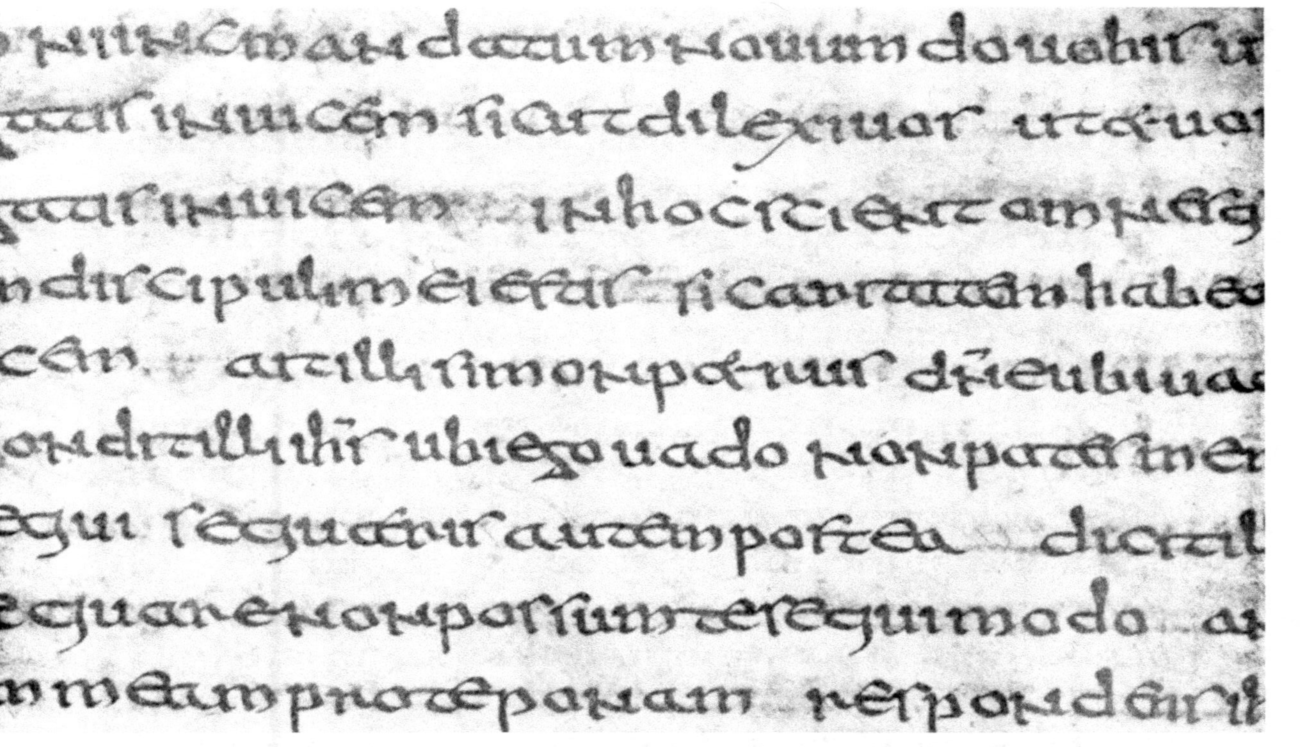

Fig. 2 Codex Usserianus Primus, early seventh century Latin gospel book, Dublin: Trinity Colleg MS. A. 4, 15.

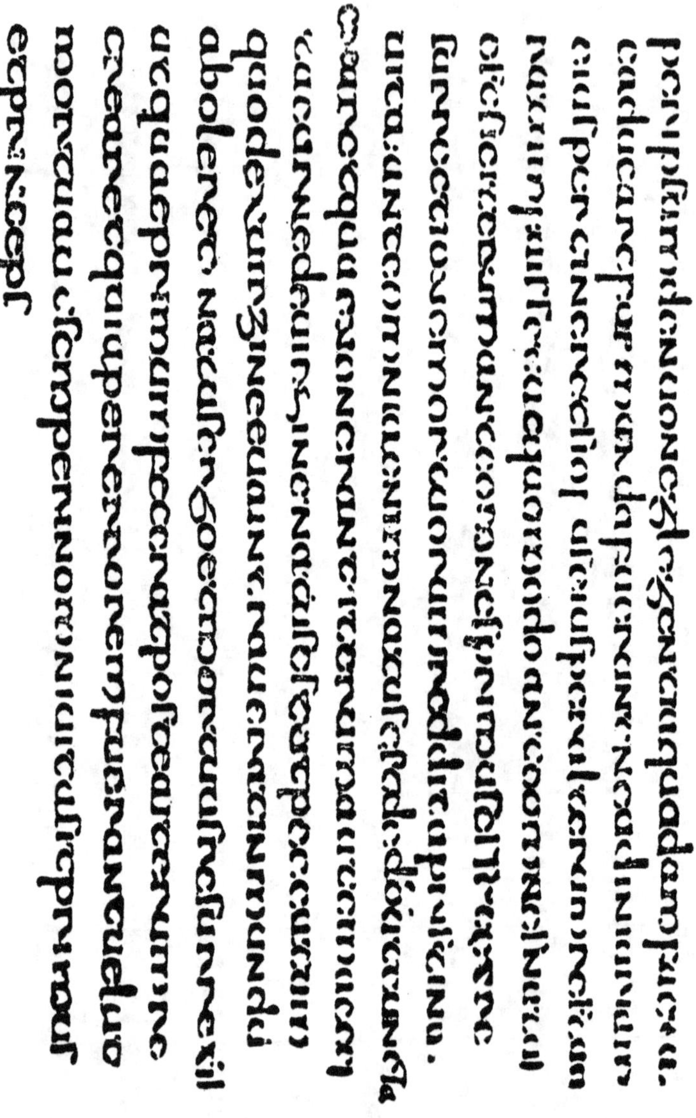

Fig. 3 Biblical commentary, sixth century.

favour and became the model for the national hand. For purposes of comparison, we may look at a facsimile (Fig. 3) from the theological manuscript in half uncial at Monte Cassino, given in Zangemeister and Wattenbach's *Exempla* (tab. 53), an example of a calligraphic style, and, although somewhat defaced, an admirable pattern of this kind of writing in the middle of the sixth century. It was undoubtedly manuscripts of this description which the creators of the Irish hand had before them when they set about forming that beautiful early character which was destined to have the longest life of any national handwriting in Western Europe. How early this style of writing was introduced into Ireland we have no authority for deciding, but it is hardly possible that the connection between the Roman half-uncial and the native hand can date back to a period much earlier than the earliest extant Irish MSS. The likeness between the two scripts is too close to admit of parallel descents from a remote origin. The Irish hand might, as we know it afterwards did, have become stereotyped at an early period, and thus might have continued almost changeless for a long time. But we know that this was not the case with the Roman hands.

In Ireland, then, in the seventh century a beautiful national hand founded on the Roman half-uncial had been created; and it is remarkable how rapidly it expanded, resulting in the production of such sumptuous volumes as the Book of Kells of the close of the seventh century.

The history of the introduction of the Irish hand into England may be briefly stated. In consequence of the conversion of Oswald, who became king of Northumberland in the year 635, and who had accepted Christianity during his exile in the Irish monastery of Iona, a foundation of St Columba, Aidan, a monk of that house, came into England, and, as the founder of the

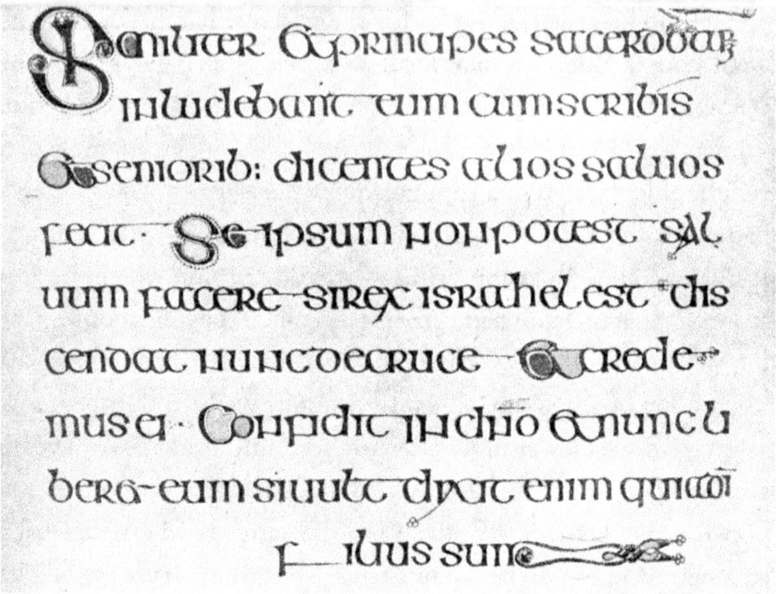

Fig. 4 The Book of Kells, seventh century, Dublin: Trinity College MS 58.

Similiter et principes et sacerdotu*m*
inludebant eum cum scribis
et seniorib*us* dicentes alios saluos
fecit. Se ipsum non potest sal
uum facere si rex israhel est dis
cendat nunc de cruce et crede
mus ei. Confiidit in d*omi*no et nunc li
beret eum si uult dixit enim quia d*ei*
filius sum

Northumbrian church, established his see at Lindisfarne, which became a centre of learning and a great school for the production of manuscripts. At first, naturally, the style of writing was nothing more than the Irish style transferred to English soil; and the writing produced in England is not very distinguishable from that of purely Irish manuscripts. Still, a certain difference does by degrees become observable, the wider range offered to the younger hand bringing it under influence denied to its forerunner.

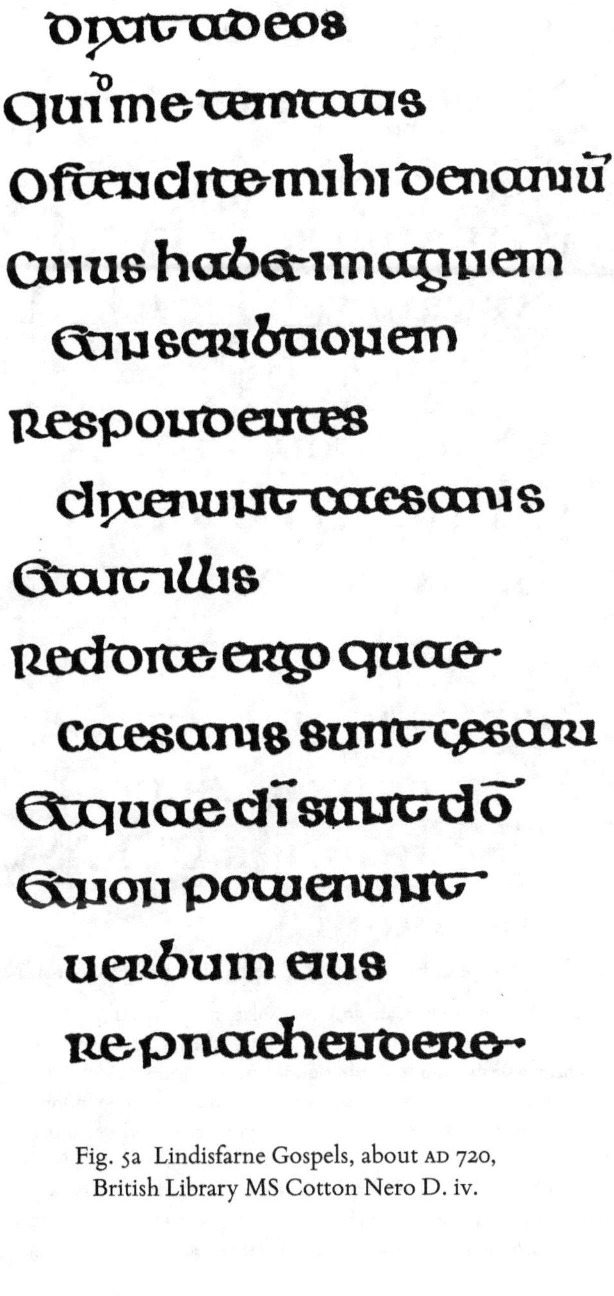

dixit ad eos
quid me temptatis
ostendite mihi denariū
cuius habet imaginem
et inscribtionem
respondentes
dixerunt caesaris
et ait illis
reddite ergo quae
caesaris sunt cęsari
et quae dī sunt dō
et non potuerunt
uerbum eius
repraehendere

Fig. 5a Lindisfarne Gospels, about AD 720,
British Library MS Cotton Nero D. iv.

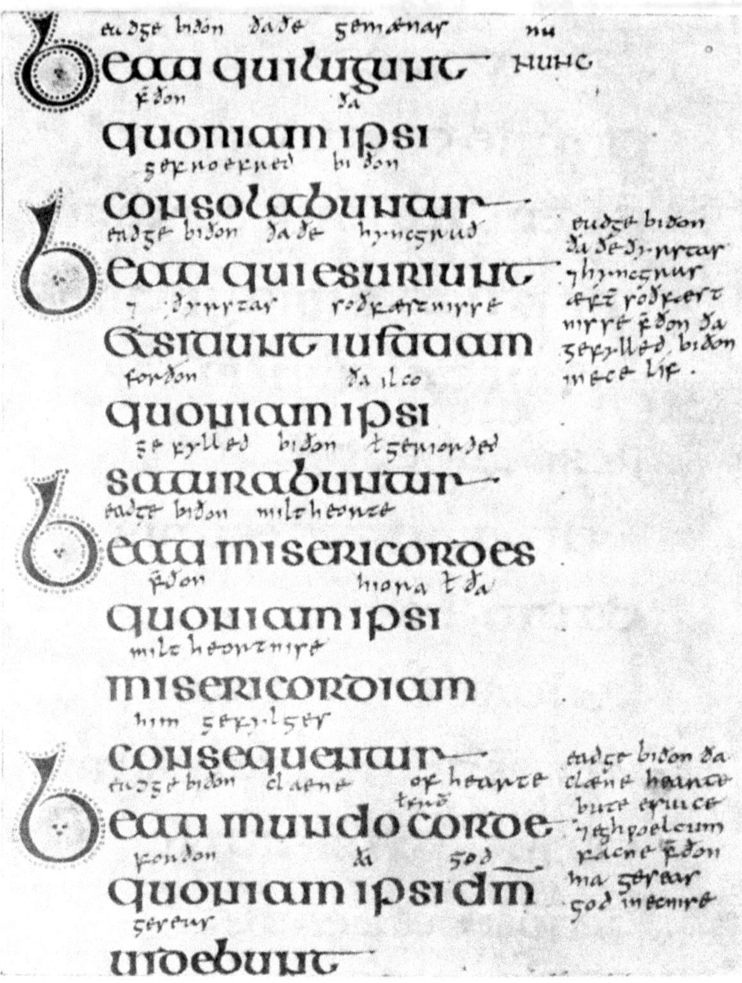

Fig. 5b Lindisfarne Gospels, c. 720, British Library MS Cotton Nero D. iv.

Beati qui lugunt nunc | quoniam ipsi | consolabuntur | Beati qui esuriunt | et sitiunt iustitiam | quoniam ipsi | saturabuntur | Beati misericordes | quoniam ipsi | misericordiam | consequentur | Beati mundo corde | quoniam ipsi d*eum* | videbunt || [gloss:] eadge biðon ða ðe gemænas nú | *for*ðon ða | gefroefred biðon | eadge biðon ða ðe hyncgrað | ⁊ ðrystas soðfæstnisse | forðon ða ilco | gefylled biðon *vel* geriorded | eadge biðon miltheorte | *for*ðon hiora *vel* ða | miltheortnise | him gefylges | eadge biðon claene of *vel* fro*m* hearte | forðon ða god | geseas || eadge biðon ða ðe ðyrstas ⁊ hynegras æft*er* soðfæstnisse *for*ðon ða gefylled biðon in ece líf || eadge biðon ða clæne hearte bute esuice ⁊ eghwoelcum facne *for*ðon hia geseas god in ecnise

To illustrate the Irish style of writing as practised at Lindisfarne, we naturally have recourse (Figures 5a and 5b) to that wonderful book the Lindisfarne Gospels or Durham Book, now in the Cotton collection of manuscripts in the British Library, written in perfectly formed half-uncial letters. The volume contains the four Gospels in Latin, and is stated by early tradition to have been written by Eadfrith, Bishop of Lindisfarne from 698 to 721, in honour of St. Cuthbert, who died in 687. The period of the manuscript may be therefore placed about the year 720. But it is not only for its writing, but also for its elaborate ornamentation, chiefly of the Irish character, that this volume is so famous. The same fine type of writing is to be seen in other less perfect manuscripts still preserved at Durham, and in a few fragmentary examples in other places, such, for instance, as MS Harley 2965 (see front cover) in the British Library, which contains Lessons and Prayers in writing of the eighth century, and which formerly belonged to Winchester. But such a sumptuous style could not be maintained as a literary hand for more general purposes. Like the fine uncial hand used under similar conditions on the Continent, it was bound to give way before the requirements of literature which needed a more expeditious means of expression. The lack of later examples of English origin seems to prove that it practically soon ceased to be cultivated in this island, and a more convenient and lighter form of calligraphic writing superseded it as a literary hand, formed, however, on the same lines as the older hand.

At this point it will be convenient to break the thread of our sketch of the English national hand to take a brief survey of the handwriting which, as noticed above, entered into some competition with the Irish form of writing as a literary hand in this island. This is the Roman uncial hand, which, in the early centuries

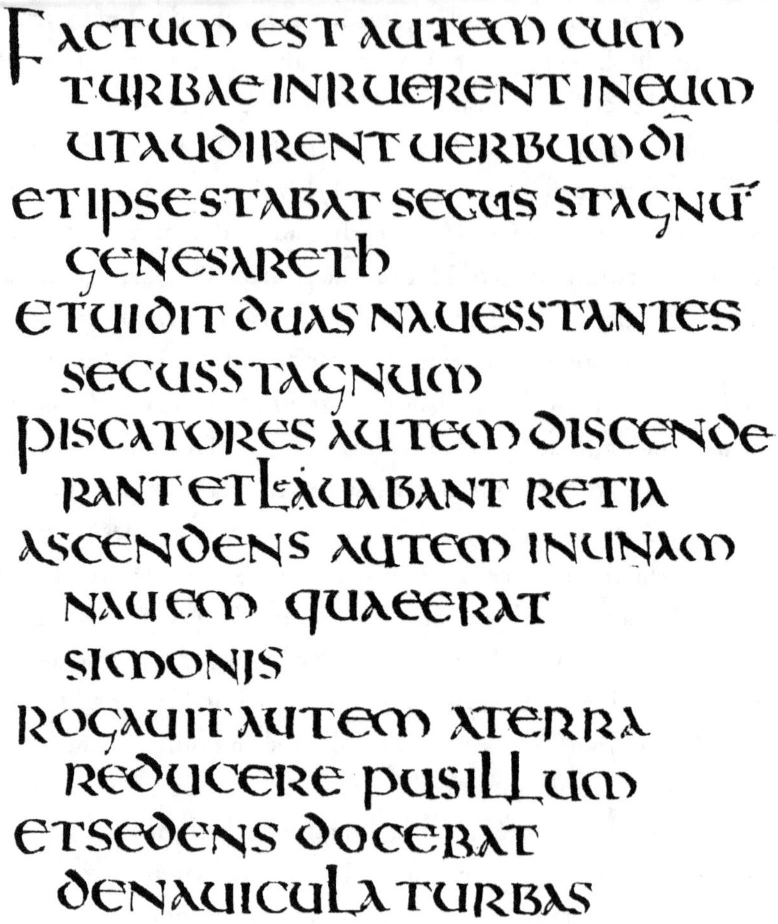

FACTUM EST AUTEM CUM
TURBAE INRUERENT INEUM
UTAUDIRENT UERBUM DĪ
ETIPSESTABAT SECUS STAGNŪ
GENESARETH
ETUIDIT DUAS NAUESSTANTES
SECUSSTAGNUM
PISCATORES AUTEM DISCENDE
RANTETLAUABANT RETIA
ASCENDENS AUTEM INUNAM
NAUEM QUAEERAT
SIMONIS
ROGAUITAUTEM ATERRA
REDUCERE PUSILLUM
ETSEDENS DOCEBAT
DENAUICULA TURBAS

Fig. 6 Codex Amiatinus, commisioned by Ceolfrid in AD 692, and now in Florence, Bibioteca Laurenziana

of the Middle Ages, became the recognized literary hand on the Continent, for manuscripts written in a calligraphic or sumptuous style. This hand appears, so far as surviving examples provide us with the means of forming a judgement, to have effected a footing at the two extreme ends of the country, in Northumberland and in Kent; with this difference, however, that, while in the north it seems never to have lost its character as a purely foreign hand (being in fact, as we have good reason to believe, in some instances at least, practised there by foreign scribes), in the south it passed beyond that stage and was adopted to some extent by native scribes. The most famous example of this style of writing, of northern origin, is the Codex Amiatinus (Fig. 6) at Florence, a great MS of the Bible written by order of Ceolfrid, Abbot of Jarrow in Northumbria in 692, who died in 716 on his way to Rome, where he intended to present the volume to the Pope. This writing is altogether of the type which we should call Italian, and there can be little hesitation in attributing it to foreign scribes, whom we know Ceolfrid to have introduced into this country. It is more interesting for our purpose to turn to the south and to see what success the uncial hand met with there. Beyond Canterbury, the city where it was probably introduced directly from abroad, it appears to have made no progress at all; but still the examples which have survived prove that uncial writing was here practised by native scribes. This is very evident from MS Cotton Vespasian A. i, containing the psalter, written about the year 700 with a later interlinear English gloss (Fig. 7). The forms of the uncial letters of this text are so manifestly imitative, that even taken by themselves their native origin cannot be doubted, but, in addition, the character of the decoration makes the provenance of the MS quite certain. It belonged to the monastery of St Augustine, Canterbury, and was no doubt produced there.

But foreign styles of writing could not stand against the more expeditious native hands which had now been established throughout the country, working down from the north. They totally disappear, and leave the field in possession of the round

Fig. 7 Eighth-century psalter with later Old English interlinear gloss, British Library MS Cotton Vespasian A.i.

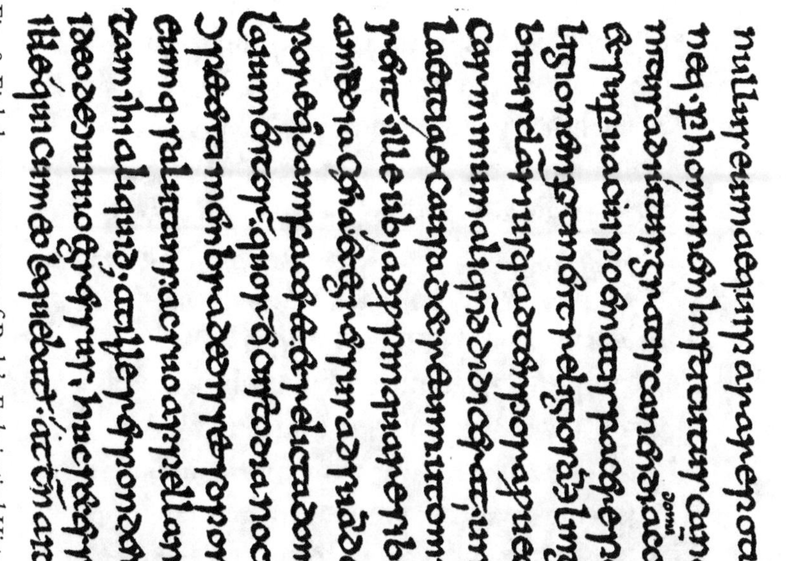

Fig. 8 Eighth-century copy of Bede's *Ecclesiastical History*, Cambridge University Library MS Kk. 5. 16

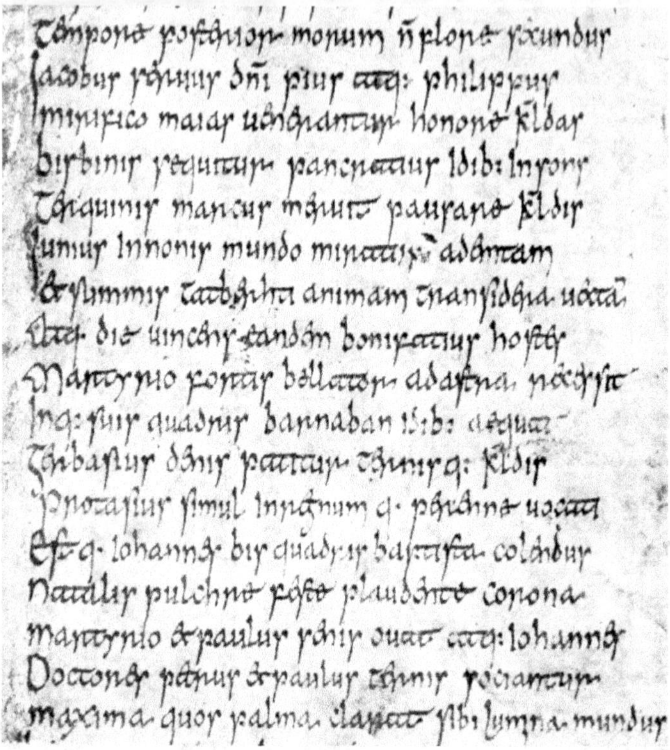

Fig. 9 Bede's *Martyrologium Poeticum,* ninth century, Bodleian MS Digby 63.

Tempore posterior morum n*on* flore secundus
Iacobus servus d*omin*i pius atq*ue* philippus
Mirifico maias venerantur honore k*alen*das
His binis sequitur pancratius idib*us* insons
Ter quinis marcus meruit pausare k*alen*dis
Iunius in nonis mundo miratur ademtam
Et summis tatberhti animam transidera vect*am*
Atq*ue* die vincens eandem bonifatius hostes
Martyrio fortis bellator ad astra recessit
Inq*ue* suis quadris barnaban idib*us* aequat
Gerbasius denis patitur ternisq*ue* k*alen*dis
Protasius simul in regnumq*ue* perenne vocati
Estq*ue* iohannes bis quadris baptista calendus
Natalis pulchre feste plaudente corona
Martyrio et paulus senis ovat atq*ue* iohannes
Doctores petrus et paulus ternis sociantur
Maxima quos palma clarat sibi lumina mundus

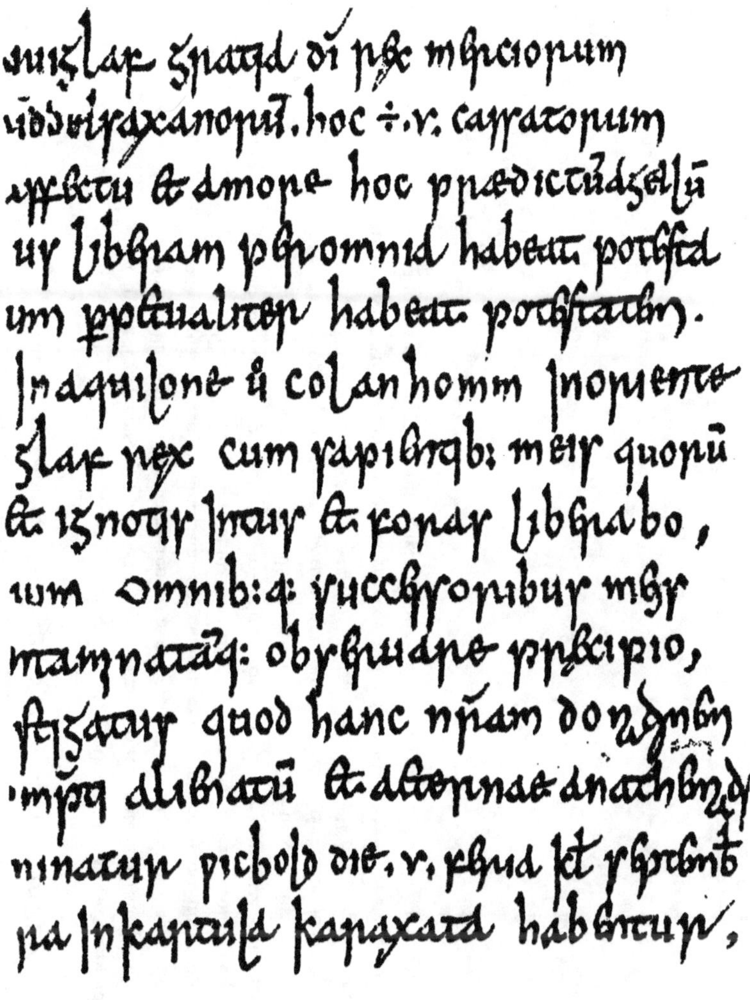

Fig. 10 Mercian charter (a section), AD 831, British Library MS Cotton Aug. II, 94.

Fig. 11 Exchange charter, AD 812, between Cynewulf, King of the Mercians, and Wulfred, Archbishop of Canterbury, Canterbury Cathedral Archives, MS CCA-DCc-ChAnt/C/1278.

IN nomine d*e*i summi regis aeterni . anno *quoque* incarnationis d*e*i et salvatoris mundi . dccc° . xii°—
anno uulfredi archiepiscopi vii° . INter alios quoque d*e*o adnuente bonarum rerum —
tationes agellorum ambobus conpetentius in orientalibus cantiae partibus sapientibus —
ratione aliquam terrae partiunculam . hoc e*st* duarum manentium in loco ubi sueord —
Seu in alio loco mediam partem unius mansiunculae id e*st* an ioclet ab incolis ibi ecghean —
praetio ab uulfhardo praesbyt*e*ro iam dudum aeðelheardi bonae memoriae arc*hi*epis—
ipse illam terram conparare et possedere optenuit . id e*st* ut iure hereditario per —
sive ab omni opere puplico aedificiorum aut in quolibet ducatu perenniter libera f—
UNde igitur xr*ist*i gratia uulfred arc*hi*episc*opus* eandem terram sibi tam propriam et quam—
prạ̊curavit . Atque etiam insuper sic regi coenuulfo dare atq*ue* ad rei puplic[ae bona]e co —
mutatione verbi gratia istorum qui in partibus suburbanis regis oppidulo fefres[ham]

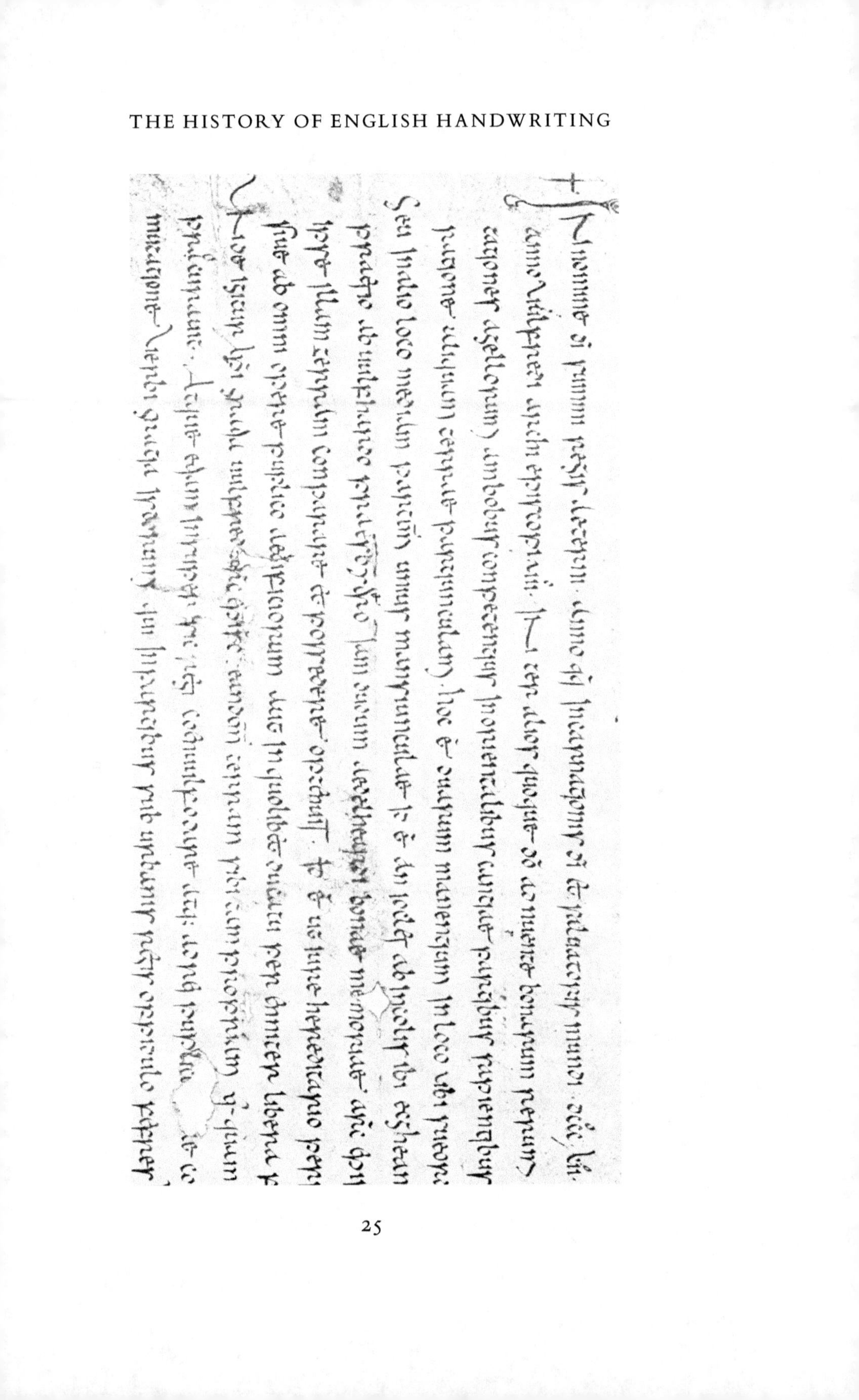

Fig. 12 Charter of Ethelberht of Kent, exchanging land in Wassingwelle (Westwell), AD 858, British Library MS. Cotton Aug. II, 66.

regnante in perpetuum d*omi*ne d*e*o n*ost*ro omnipotente sabaot ego eðelbe[arht]—
divinorumq*ue* p*er*sonaru*m* liventi animo dabo et cocedo me fideli—
in illa loco ubi wasngwelle nominat*ur* in bicissitudinem alterius ter[re]—
wellan ego eðelbearht ab omni servitute regali operis eternaliter—
ham hec sunt etenim marisci q*ue* ad eandem terram rite ac recte p*er*ti[nent]—
to wii ⁊ to leanaham ⁊ et febresham .i. sealtern, ⁊ .ii. wenagang mid cynin[ges wenu*m*]—
an wiwarawic .xxx. statera kasei et item .x. statera in alia wiwarawic—
lan his notissimis terminib*us* antiq*u*itus circu*m* iacentibus ab occide[nte]—
cuðrices dun heregeðeland ab oriente wighelmes landa meritie—
nentia una an wassingwellan alia an hwite celdan hec sunt pasc[ua] —
lamburnanden orricesden teligden stanehtandenn et illa silvas —

+ Regnante inperpetuum dño đo nño omnipotenti sabaoth. ego eðel be
diuino p(re)mium q(uae)r(ens) p(er)sona p(ro)p(ri)a libentia animo dabo et concedo meo fideli
ƿullafo co(miti) ubi ƿasingƿelle nominat(ur) inbicissitudinem alterius terr(ae)
ƿellan ego eðelbearht ab omni seruitute regali operis et terr(ae)na lit(?)
ham. hec sunt et termini marisci qui ad eandem terram pertinent ac pertinent(?)
ƿorþ(?) 7 tolean na ham. ƿeobures ham. [illegible] pena ʒang(?) [illegible]
an [illegible] .xxx. [illegible] .x. [illegible]
lan his notissimis terminibus [illegible] cum [illegible] abus ab oc(?) cide(ntali)
[illegible] dun hepe ʒe ðelande ab oriente [illegible] meslandamepi(?) [illegible]
[illegible] una an [illegible] ƿasingƿellan alia an [illegible] hec sunt pasc(u)a
lambur(?) nan den [illegible] den [illegible] den [illegible] lan den [illegible] il la silua [illegible]

literary hand which has already been described, and of the more cursive pointed hand, which now claims our attention.

It is remarkable that the growth of the cursive hand in Ireland and England was just the reverse of that of the cursive national hands of the Continent. The latter grew from the Roman cursive and were eventually moulded into shape to serve as literary hands. In Ireland the literary hand came into the country ready-made, the Roman half uncial, from which, as we have seen, the literary Irish hand was copied, being a set hand employed for literature; and the Irish cursive or pointed hand is a mere modification of the same pattern, either growing up *pari passu* with the round literary Irish hand, or even being subsequent to it. It might have been foreseen that, as soon as this pointed hand was quite developed, the greater ease and rapidity with which it could be written would ensure its superseding not only the large half-uncial hand of the early codices, but also that lighter round hand which has been referred to. And, following the law that a new hand always appears at its best in the earliest stages of its literary existence, the pointed hand is of a particularly fine type in manuscripts of the eighth century. The famous MS of Bede's *Ecclesiastical History,* in the University Library of Cambridge, is probably the finest MS extant of this class and of this period. It exhibits (Fig. 8) the Anglo-Saxon pointed hand of the middle of the eighth century in its most perfect form-the chief characteristic of the letters being their handsome breadth and excellent formation, quite free from any exaggeration.

This pointed or cursive hand, then, became the most widely accepted style in the eighth and ninth centuries, during which period it generally maintained its excellence. The fortunate survival of a fairly large number of charters of this time enables us to follow

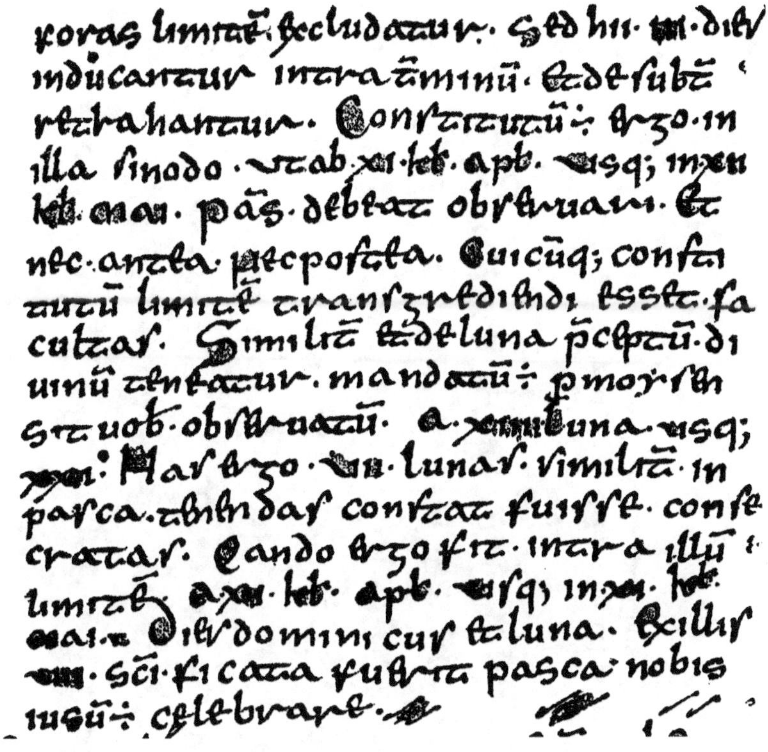

Fig. 13 Paschal computations, ninth century, Bodleian MS. Digby 63.

fora limit*em* . excludatur. Sed hii .iii. dies
inducantur intra t*er*minu*m* . et desubt*er*
retrahantur . Constitutu*m est* ergo . in
illa sinodo . ut ab .xi. kl. Ap*rilis* . usq*ue* in .xii.
kl. Mai. Pas*ca* debeat obseruari . Et
nec . antea . nec postea. Cuicu*m*q*ue* consti
tutu*m* limit*em* transgrediendi esset . fa
cultas . Similit*er* et de luna p*re*ceptu*m* di
uinum teneatur . mandatu*m est per* moysen
sit vob*is* . observatu*m* . a .xiiii. luna . usq*ue*
xxi. Has ergo .vii. lunas . similit*er* . in
pasca. tenendas constat fuisse . conse
crateas . Quando ergo fit . intra illu*m*
limit*em* . a .xii. kl. Ap*rilis* . usq*ue* in .xi. kl.
Mai .v. Dies dominicus et luna. Ex illis
viii. *sanct*ificata fuerit pasca . nobis
insu*m est* cęlebrare .

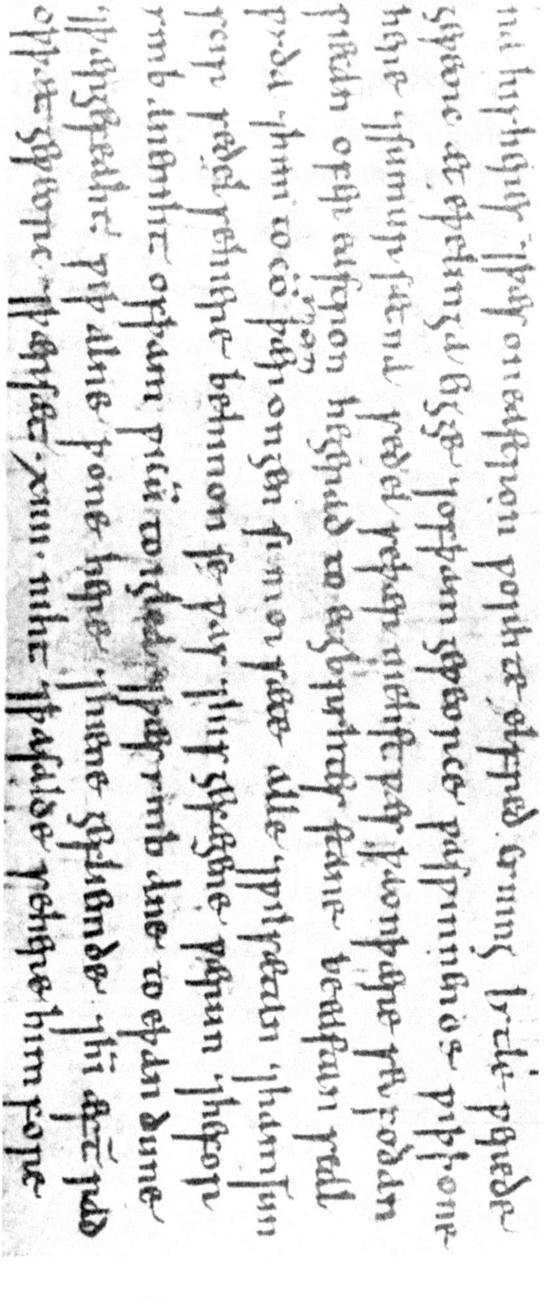

Fig. 14 Anglo-Saxon Chronicle written at Winchester c. 891, Cambridge: Corpus Christi, Parker Library MS 173.

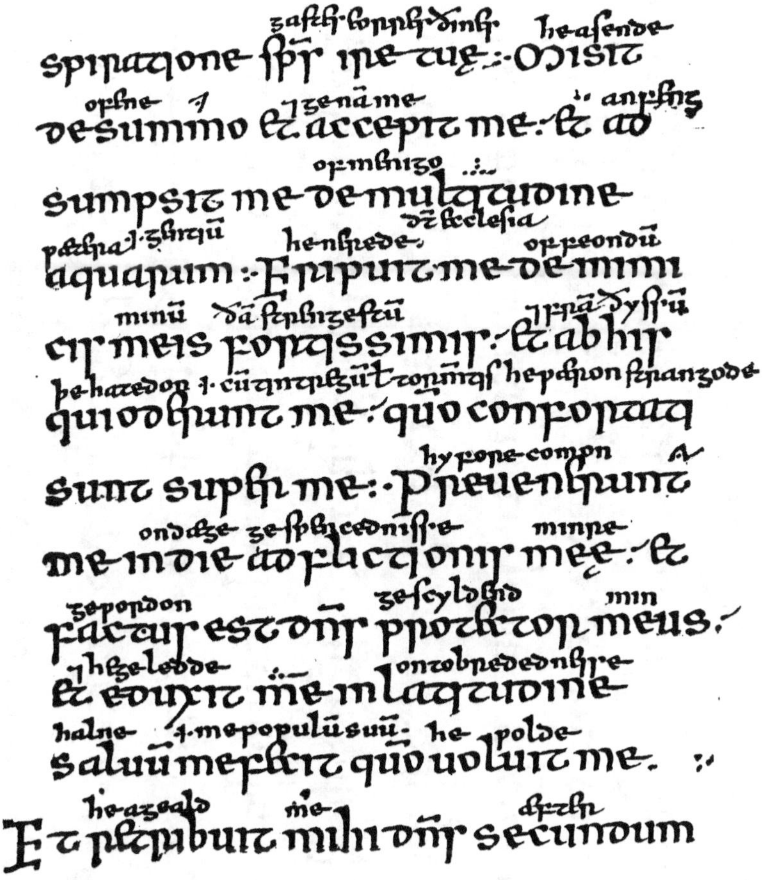

Fig. 15 Regius Psalter, 10th century, British Library MS Royal 2 B v.

Fig. 16 Anglo-Saxon poetry from the Exeter Book, about AD 950, Exeter: Cathedral Library MS 3501.

Fig. 17 Sherborne Pontifical, about AD 992–5, Paris: Bibliothèque Nationale de France MS Lat. 943.

the course that it followed with some approach to precision, and, further, we can even trace the distinctive character that it assumed in different kingdoms of the Heptarchy. Mercia, above all other kingdoms, seems to have cultivated artistic feeling, and there we see in practice a particularly beautiful kind of writing, very light and graceful. A charter of Wiglaf of Mercia of the year 831 (British Library MS Cotton Aug. ii. 94) is an example of this beautiful hand. Here (Fig. 10) we have a document a hundred years later than the Cambridge Bede, and we mark the change. Instead of the breadth which characterized the writing of that manuscript, we see in this hand a tendency to compression, which, however, when combined with the light touch and fine strokes, is very effective in appearance.

Turning to another kingdom of the Heptarchy, the rising kingdom of Wessex, we find quite a different class of hand; a heavy, rugged, and rather ill-formed hand, quite wanting in the beauty and elegant touch of the writing of Mercia. This style of writing in its cursive form may be seen in several specimens printed in the series of Anglo-Saxon Charters in the British Library. And it was not altogether confined to Wessex. When Kent fell under the dominion and influence of that kingdom, naturally scribes from Wessex were employed there as well as in the west. The Cotton Charter, Aug. ii. 66, of Ethelberht of Kent, AD 858 (Fig. 12), is a good typical example of the style. From other extant Kentish charters it seems that that kingdom followed now the Mercian type, now the Wessex type; it does not appear to have had a distinctive character of its own. There is in the Bodleian Library a volume of collections relating to the paschal cycle and other computations (Digby MS 63), written at Winchester in the middle of the ninth century, which is an excellent example (Fig. 13) of

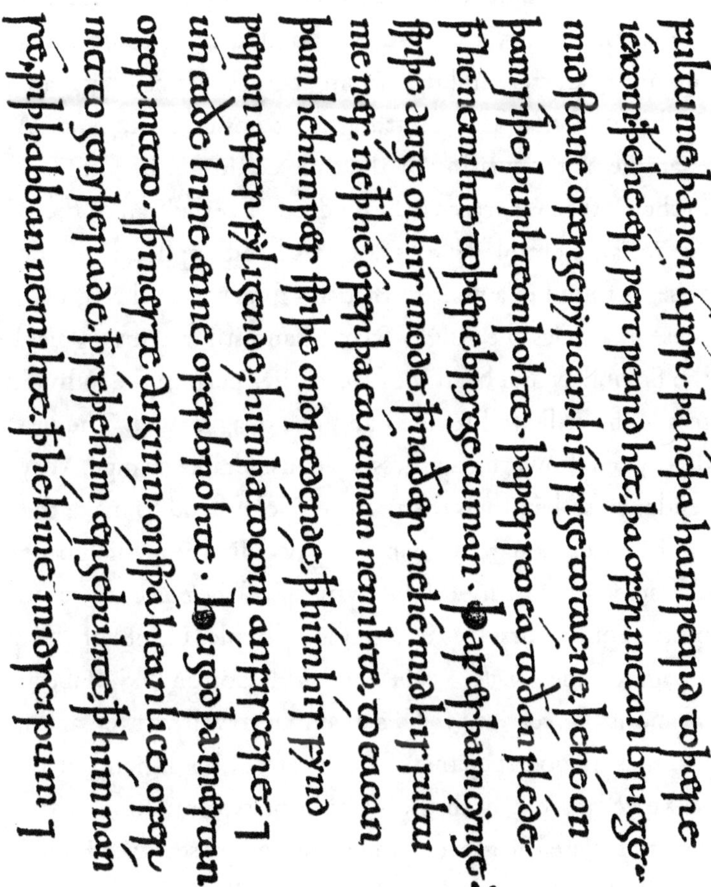

Fig. 18 *Anglo-Saxon Chronicle*, written at Abingdon in about AD 1045, British Library, MS Cotton Tiberius B. i.

the Wessex hand put to literary uses. Here of course the natural irregularity of the hand is kept within bounds, but one at once recognizes the local character in such letters as the 's' and 't'.

But necessarily these local distinctions gradually disappeared as the whole of England was gathered under one power. Passing into the tenth century, we find the pointed hand assuming a rather squarer character, and developing certain forms which are guides to the palæographer in settling the dates of documents. A better example of the writing of the time could not be found than that in the Cotton Charter viii. 16, a deed of Æthelstan of the year 931. Again, an example (Fig.15) of this hand applied to literary purposes is found in a psalter (British Library, Royal 2 B. v.). In both these examples the Anglo-Saxon hand still retains a great deal of the flexibility and beauty of the earlier period; the individual letters being still well formed and not exaggerated. The next hundred years, however, witnesses a considerable change. Very soon a tendency to lengthen the vertical strokes, and to make the bodies of the letters square, is manifest – peculiarities which become the characteristic features of the writing of the eleventh century. We must confine ourselves to a single example (Fig.18) of this period, a page of the *Anglo-Saxon Chronicle,* Cotton MS, Tiberius B. i, of about the year 1045. This example is well written and must be taken as a good specimen of the careful book-hand of the time. If we compare it with the writing of two hundred years earlier, we appreciate the great change that had passed over English writing. Unlike her secluded sister-island, Ireland, where the native hand, uninfluenced by contact from without, held its own way and passed into a stereotyped form, England was more or less in touch with the Continent; and particularly in the Anglo-Saxon writing of the eleventh century one cannot fail to recognize the

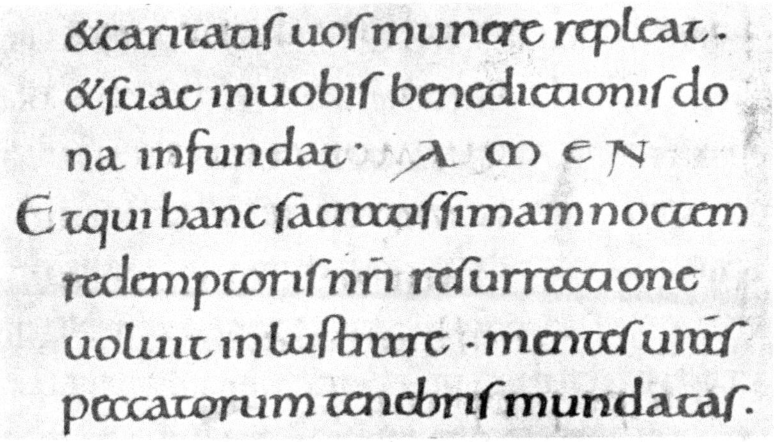

Fig. 19 Benedictional of St Æthelwold, AD 963–984,
British Library MS Add. 495598.

et caritatis uos munere repleat
et suae in uobis benedictionis do
na infundat. Amen
Et qui hanc sacratissimam noctem
redemptoris n*ost*ri ressurrectione
uoluit inlustrare . mentes u*est*ras
peccatorum tenebris mundatas.

result of the influence of the handwriting practised across the Channel. There is in the native eleventh century hand an element of the feeling of this foreign hand – not traceable, indeed, in the actual forms of letters, but in that undefinable expression which we call character.

This foreign influence had been at work for some time; for even in the tenth century we find that the foreign minuscule of the Carolingian type had already been partially and locally adopted for Latin texts and for liturgical books. A notable example is the Benedictional of St Æthelwold, Bishop of Winchester from 963 to 984 (Fig. 19), formerly in possession of the Duke of Devonshire [Now British Library MS Add. 49598] – the most elaborately-

ambitum quasi pgule desiderii. sese ad ima sum
mittunt; Unde & bene subdit. & uniuersa idola
domus israhel depicta erant in pariete; Scrip
tum quippe est. & auaritia que ē idolorum
seruitus; Recte ergo post animalia idola de-
scribunt. quia & si honesta actione nonnulli q̄si
a terra se erigunt. ambitione tam̄ inhonesta. se-
met ipsos ad terrā deponunt; Bene autē dicitur
depicta erant. quia dū exteriorū rerū intrinse
cus species attrahunt. quasi in corde depingitur.
quic quid fictis imaginibus deliberando cogitatur;
Notandum itaq· est quia prius foramen in pariete.
ac deinde ostiū cernitur. & tunc demum occulta
abhominatio demonstrat. quia nimirum uniuscui
que peccati prius signa forinsecus. deinde ianua
apte iniquitatis ostendit. & tunc demū omne malū
quod intꝰ latet aperitur; Nonnulla autē sunt lenit
arguenda. nā cū non malitia sed sola ignorantia ł infir
mitate delinquit. pfecto necesse ē ut magno mode
ramine ipsa delicti correptio temperet; Cuncti

Fig. 20 Gregory's *Pastoral Care,* Oxford: Bodleian Library, MS Bodley 708, early eleventh century.

ornamented Anglo-Saxon manuscript of this time in existence. Another example is a Troparium, in the Bodleian Library, which may be of the end of the tenth century, and in any case is earlier than the year 1016. But in the foreign hand thus introduced – only, however, at such centres as Winchester and probably Canterbury, where the influence of foreign ecclesiastics would first show itself – it is interesting to see how the native character reacts upon it. An instance of a mixed hand is seen in a manuscript of Aldhelm *de Virginitate,* at Lambeth [MS 200, Part II], of the latter part of the tenth century. And perhaps a still better example (Fig. 20) is to be found in a MS of Gregory's *Pastoral Care,* which belonged to Exeter, now in the Bodleian Library. The manuscript is of the beginning of the eleventh century, of English penmanship, the most noticeable letter being the 'g', which is a kind of compromise between the Carolingian and Anglo-Saxon forms.

We might speculate upon the line that English writing would have followed had there been no Norman Conquest of England, and we might even assume without much hesitation that undoubtedly the foreign Carolingian minuscule, so simple in its forms, would in any case have been widely adopted, and would as a book-hand have not improbably almost superseded in course of time the native writing. But the latter would probably have held its own as a charter-hand and as the form of writing for vernacular manuscripts, but still progressing in course of time to a still nearer assimilation to the foreign cast of writing than that which we detect in the Anglo-Saxon writing in the reign of Edward the Confessor. But the Conquest came, and the fate of Anglo-Saxon writing was sealed. From this time forward the history of English writing practically runs with the history of the writing generally of Western Europe. With the conquerors came Norman scribes.

Fig. 21 King Alfred's translation of Gregory's *Pastoral Care,* 11th century, Cambridge: Trinity College R. 5. 22 (III), fol. 112 v.

gescendad · þoñ feallað þa hean hwommas þe hi ahebbaþ for þere
twyfealdesse þæs unrihtan wærscipes · þurh rihtlicne cwide ·
⁊ dom · weorðaþ ðoñ ofdune aworpene · ~Ðæt on oþre wisan synt
to manigenne þa halan ⁊ on oþre ða únhalan: /

ON OÐRE · Wisan synt tó manienne þa truman ·
ón oðre þa untruman; Ða truman synt tó manien
ne þǽt hí gewilnigen mid þæs lichoman trūnesse · þǽt hím ne losige
sé hǽle þǽs modes · þyles him þe wyrs sie · gif hí þa rumnesse
þære godes gife hým tó unytte gehwyrfað · ⁊ þyles hi sæþþan
gegearnien swa mycelre hæfigre wyte · swa hie nú ægeleaslicor ·
⁊ unrihtlicor brucaþ þære myldheortlican godes gife: / For
þǣ synt to manienne þa halan · þæt hie ne forhycgen · þæt hí
hér ón worulde on þære hwylendlican hælo him geearnigen
þa ecean tida; Swa sc̄s paulus sprǽc · þa þa he cwæþ; Ecce nunc
tēus acceptabile: ecce nunc dies salutis; Nu is heorsūnisse
tima · ⁊ nu synt hælnesse dagas; Eac synt to manienne þa
halan · þæt hi gode wilnigen to lycienne þa hwyle þe hie mægen ·
þyles hí æft ne magon þoñ hí wyllan · forþon wæs gespræcen þurh

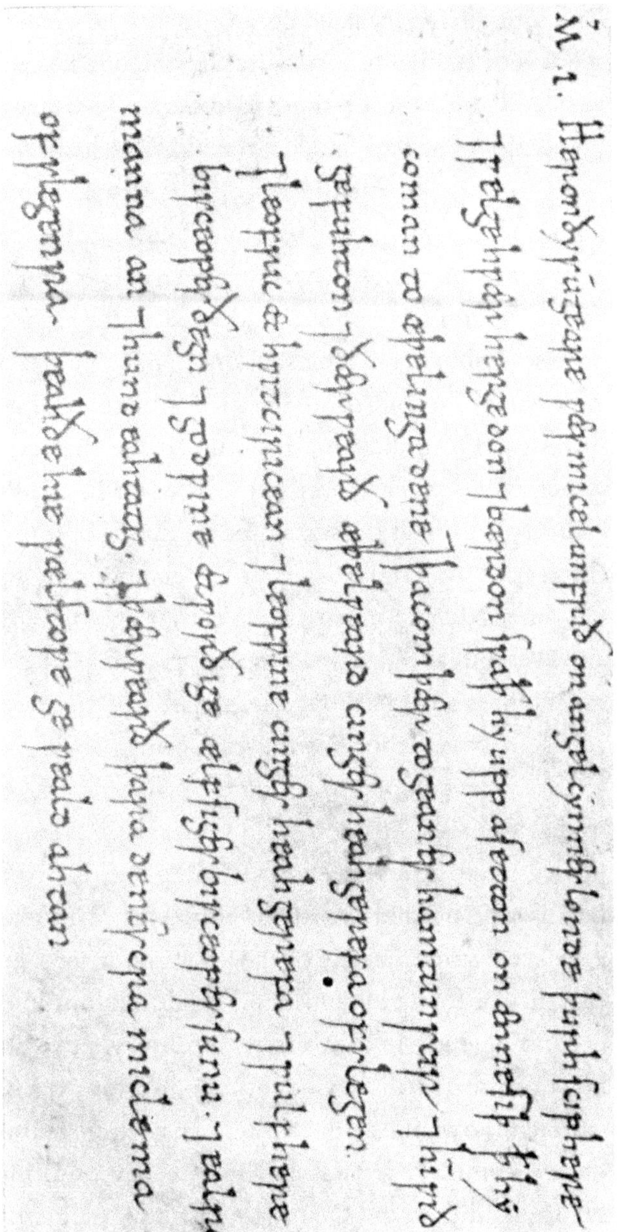

Fig. 22 *Anglo-Saxon Chronicle*, about 1001, Cambridge: Corpus Christi, Parker Library, MS 173.

The foreign literary hand became the literary hand of the writing schools of the English monasteries; the official Norman hand superseded the hand of the Anglo-Saxon charters. Still, with the blending of the two nations, the Norman hand could not remain foreign. The Conquest itself could not have drawn an absolutely hard and fast line, and there must have still remained a certain continuity of things. The English character which we can trace in the foreign style partially adopted in the tenth century, as we have seen above, can almost at once be recognized in manuscripts written in England soon after the Conquest. The foreign hand introduced into the country assumed the character of roundness which seems to have been the best point in the English sense of calligraphy. But at the same time we must not forget that the close connection of England with the neighbouring countries of the Continent during the next two centuries, conduced to keep up a close resemblance between the handwritings of England, Northern France, and the Low Countries; and the freedom of intercourse between those countries, both in social and commercial relations, was the cause of interchange of literary works, and to some extent also of those who wrote them. Hence arises the difficulty often experienced of deciding the exact provenance of a manuscript of the twelfth or thirteenth century, which might have been written in any of the three countries; hence also the occurrence of foreign manuscripts produced for the English market, not infrequently in the thirteenth century. Notwithstanding this, however, there still is evident the growth of the English style, and although now and again a volume may come before us which lies on the boundary separating the three handwritings of England, France, and the Low Countries, the bulk of English manuscripts are at once recognizable from their national features. Similar then in structure to the minuscule literary writing of the Continent, and yet differing from it in sentiment, the English literary hand passed through that noble and bold period of calligraphy, the twelfth century, and through that refined and elegant period, the thirteenth century, into the fourteenth century, when a new element was introduced into it, tending to mark its individuality more strongly than before.

We may now pass in review some specimens of writing of these later centuries – bearing in mind that the selection has been made chiefly with the view of showing what excellent work the English scribes were capable of producing – and it is to be observed that upon whatever part of the country we draw for our material, everywhere we find the same cultivation of a fine character of writing.

First, look at a page (Fig. 24) from Domesday Book, written in the official Chancery Hand of the Normans, the new official hand of England in the year 1086. It will at once be seen that the writing is in quite a different style from the literary or book-hand of the specimens which you have just had before you. The writing of the Domesday belongs to the class which I will call the charter-hand, which, in a later stage of development, had so great an influence on the course of the literary hand in England, as will presently be shown. A very fine example of Norman Chancery Hand is to be seen in a charter of William Rufus (Fig. 25) granting land to Battle Abbey. Some half century later than the Domesday is the Chartulary of St Swithun at Winchester, now in the British Library; a monastic book with the charters entered up in the ordinary book-hand, and interesting for its specimens of Old English, in which the boundaries of the land, according to custom, are given – written nearly a century after the Conquest (MS Add.

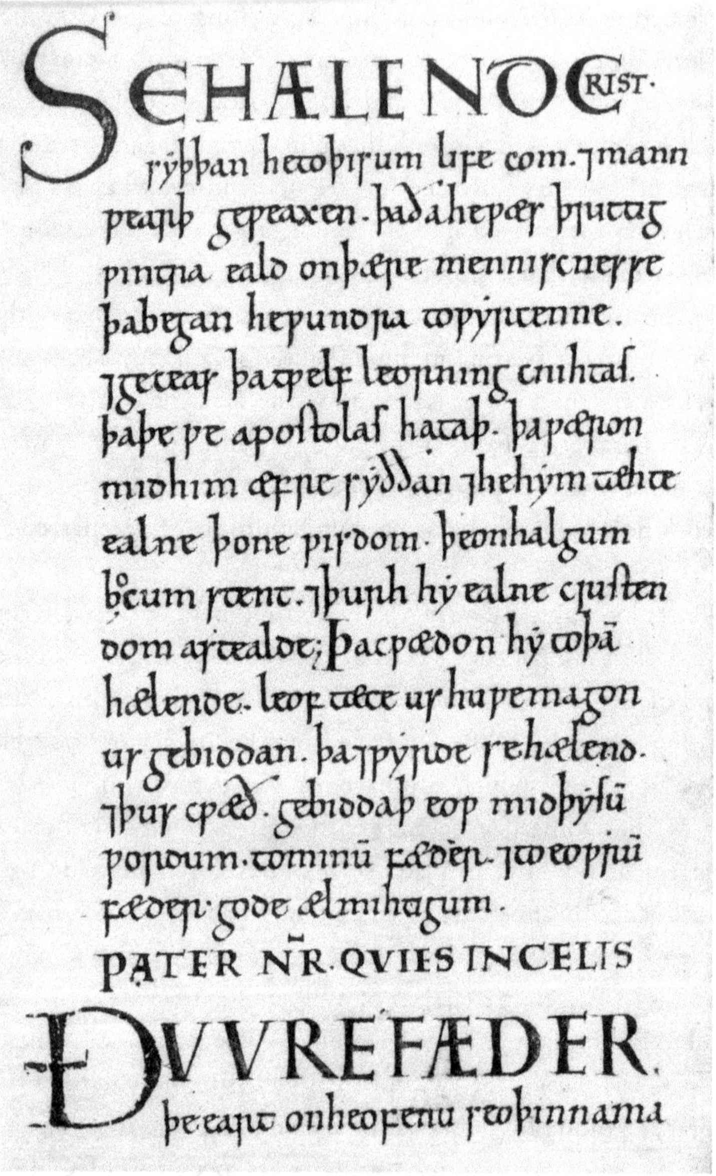

Fig. 23 Homilies, 11th century,
Cambridge: Trinity College MS B. 15. 34.

De epo ten Malgeri Lolingestone p dimi solin.
se defd. Tra. e. In dnio. e una car. 7 iii. uitti
cu. vi. bord hnt. i. car. Ibi. v. ac pti.
Totu on ualeb. lx. sol. modo. lxx. sol. De isto on ht
Rex qd ual. x. solid. Bruning tenuit de rege. E.
Isde Malgeri ten in Ferlingeha dimid iugu tre.
Tra. e. iii. bou. Ibi sunt. ii. boues. cu uno bord. 7 ii. ac pti.
Valuit 7 ual. xx. sol. Brunesune tenuit. 7 potuit
cu tra sua uertere se quo uoluit. De hoc on ten rex
qd ual. viii. sol.
Isde Malgeri ten in Pinnedene. dimid solin de epo.
Tra. e vii. bou. Ibi. e una car cu. v. uittis. 7 vi. ac pti.
Valuit 7 ual. xvi. sol. Alured tenuit T. R. E. 7 potuit
se uertere quo uoluit.
Osbnus pastforeire ten in Lolingeston dimid solin
de epo. Tra. e In dnio. e. i. car. 7 iii. uitti cu. i. bord
7 i. seruo hnt. i. car. Ibi. v. ac pti. Silua. v. porc. 7 un
molin de. xv. solid. 7 cl. anguill. Rex ht silua p nouo
dono epi. 7 ual. iii. sol. Totu on ualeb. lx. sol. Modo
lxx vii. sol. Seuuart soc tenuit. T. R. E. 7 potuit se
uertere cu tra sua quo uoluit.
Wadard ten de epo dimid solin in Ferningeha.
Tra. e. iii. car. In dnio sunt. ii. car. cu uno uitto 7 ii. cot.
7 v. seruis. Ibi dimid molin de. v. solins. 7 iiii. ac pti. Silua
v. porc. Excepto h dim solin. ten Wadard dimid iugu

Fig. 24 Domesday Book, 1086, in the new Chancery Hand introduced by the Normans.

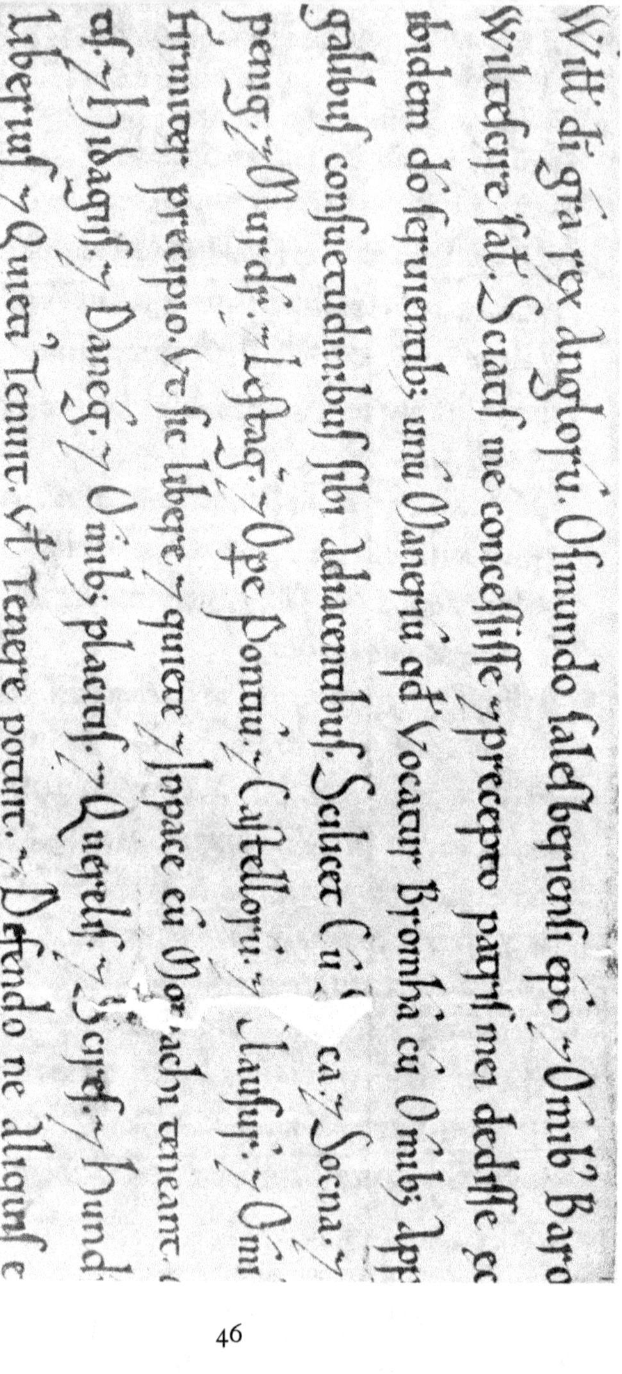

Fig. 25 Charter of William II, 1087 (?) granting the manor of Bromham to Battle Abbey, British Library MS Cotton Aug. ii. 53.

gentium populis in ciuitates
eorum & terras transtulit. Qui
quomodo accepta dei lege &
hanc ex parte seruabant:
& nichilominus eisdem quibus antea simulacris seruiebant.
Hi igitur quia ueros dei cultores
abhominabantur polliciti
sunt eis auxilium operis: ut in so-
cietatem recepti possent infer-
re dispendium. Facile autem
cuiuis patet: quia tales populi
falsos fratres. hoc est hereticos &
malos catholicos figuraliter
exprimunt. Qui hostes sunt
iude. hoc est confessionis &
laudis: quam in ecclesia domino in pre-
senti per fidem rectam & opera
fide digna offert. Hostesque
que beniamin. hoc est filii dex-
tere dei eos qui audiunt
a sorte segregauit populi fide-

Fig. 26 Bede's *Commentary on Ezra,* written for Cirencester Abbey, mid-twelfth century, British Library MS Royal 3. A. xii.

abbot Turolde ƿæs ʒehaten. ⁊ ꝥ he ƿæs sƿiðe styrne man.
⁊ ƿæs cumen þa into Stanforde mid ealle his frencisce
menn. þa ƿæs þære an cyrceƿeard Yƿare ƿæs ʒehaten.
nā þa be nihte eall þet he mihte. þet ƿæron xp̄es bec ⁊
mæssahakeles ⁊ cantelcapas ⁊ reafes ⁊ sƿilce lytles hƿat.
sƿa hƿat sƿa he mihte. ⁊ ferde sona ær dæʒ to þon̄ abbot
turolde ⁊ sæʒde hī ꝥ he sohte his ʒriðe. ⁊ cydde hī hu þa
utlaʒes sceolden cumen to burh. ꝥ he dyde eall be þære
munece ræde. þa sona on morʒen comen ealle þa utlaʒa
mid fela scipe ⁊ ƿoldon into þā mynstre. ⁊ þa munecas
ƿiðstoden ꝥ hi na mihton in cumen. þa læʒdon hi fyr
on. ⁊ forbærndon ealle þa munece huses ⁊ eall þa tun bu
ton ane huse. þa comen hi þurh fyre in æt bolhiðe ʒea
te. ⁊ þa munecas comen heō toʒanes. beaden heō ʒrið
ac hi ná rohten na þinʒ. ʒeodon into þe mynstre. clum
ben upp to þe halʒe rode. namen þa þe kynehelm of ure
drihtnes heafod eall of smeate ʒolde. namen þa þet fot
spure þe ƿæs underneðen his fote. ꝥ ƿæs eall of read
ʒolde. clumben upp to þe stepel. brohton dune ꝥ hæcce
þe þær ƿæs behid. hit ƿæs eall of gold ⁊ of seolfre. hi namen
þære tƿa ʒyldene scrines ⁊ .ix. seolferne. ⁊ hi namen
fiftene mycele roden ʒe of ʒolde ʒe of seolfre. hi namen
þære sƿa mycele ʒold ⁊ seolfre ⁊ sƿa maneʒa ʒersumas
on sceat ⁊ on scrud ⁊ on bokes sƿa nan man ne mæi oðer
tellen. sæʒdon ꝥ hi hit dyden for ðes mynstres holdscipe.
syððon ʒeden heō to scipe. ferden heom to eliʒ. betæhtan
þær þa ealla þa ʒersume. þa denescæ menn ƿændon ꝥ hi
sceoldon ofer cumen. þa frencisca men. þa todrefodon
ealle þa munekes. beleaf þær nan butan an munec he
ƿæs ʒehaten leofƿine lange. he læi seoc in þa secræman

Fig. 27 *Anglo-Saxon Chronicle,* written at Peterborough, c. 1121, Oxford: Bodleian Library MS Laud 636.

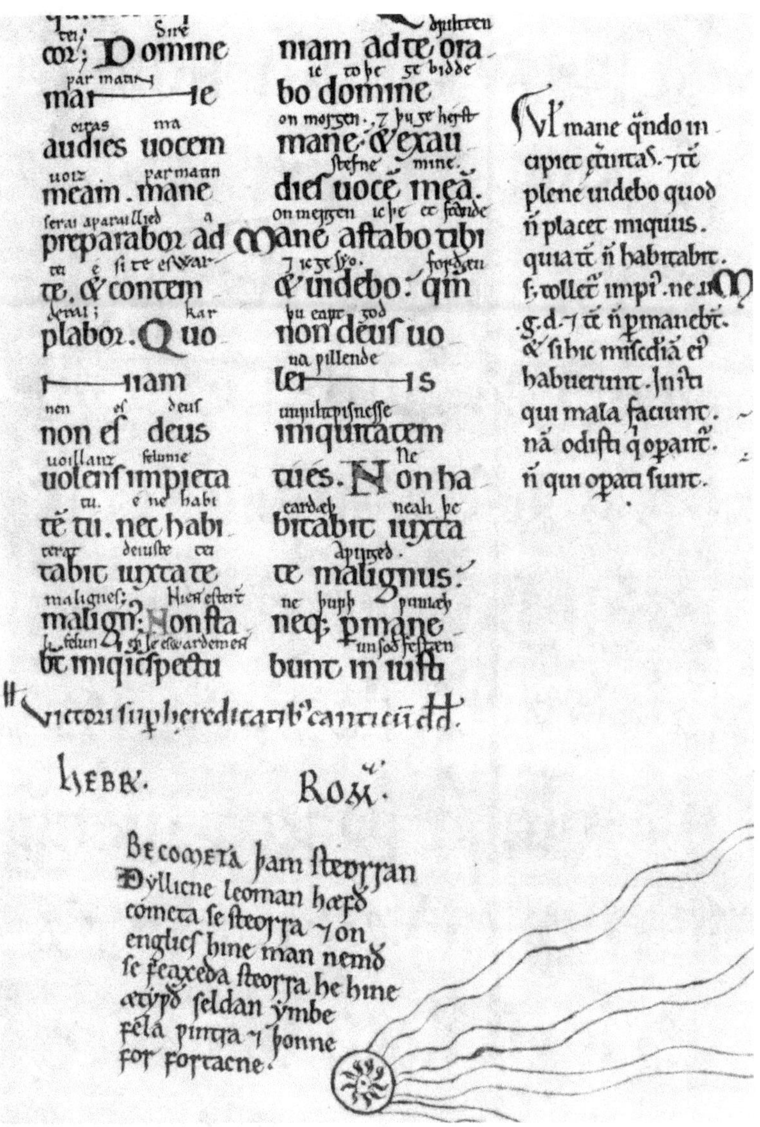

Fig. 28 Eadwine Psalter, Canterbury, circa 1155. Page shows Latin text with English and Anglo-Norman interlinear glosses and depiction of a comet with note in English. Cambridge: Trinity College MS R. 17. 1, fol. 10 r.

q͞a ꝓpeccō ē multitudinis.
Si peccauerit princeps. &
fecerit unū de pluribꝫ ꝑ-
ignorātiā. q͞d dn͞i lege ꝓhi-
bet͞. & postea intellexerit
peccm͞ suū. offeret hostiā
dn͞o. hyrcū decapris in-
maculatū. ponetq; manū
suā sup cap͞ ei͞. Cūq; imola
uerit eū iloco ubi solet
mactari holocaustū coram

Fig. 29 Leviticus, Convent of St Mary of Buildwas, Shropshire, 1176, British Library MS Harley 3038.

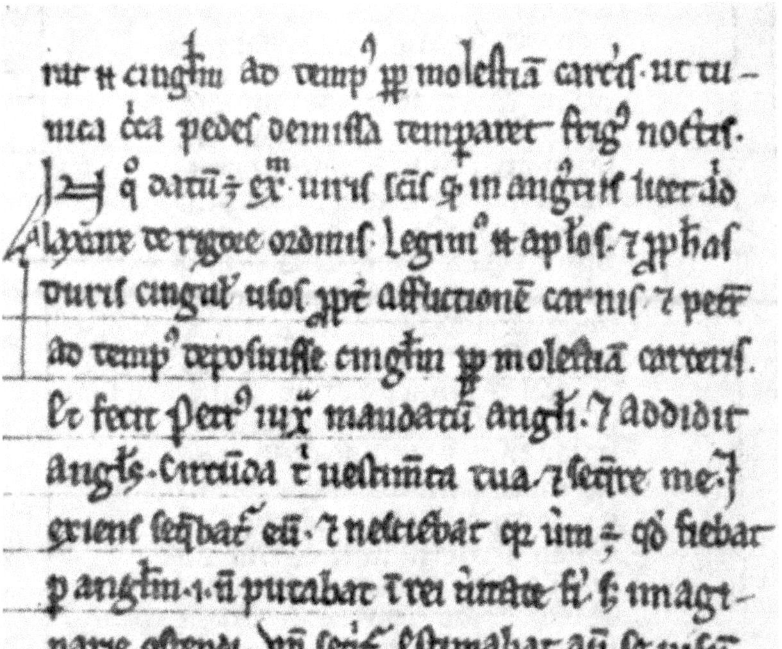

Fig. 30 Peter Comestor, *Historia Scholastica,* AD 1191–2, British Library MS Royal 7. F. iii.

Fig. 31 Bible, 1254, British Library MS Royal 1. B. xii.

Fig. 32 Peter Comestor, *Historia Scholastica,* before AD 1215, British Library MS Royal 4 D. vii.

Tractatus quidam in anglico. 169

Ich am elder þan ich wes a winter and ek on lore.
Ich welde more þan ich dude. my wyt auhte to beo more.
Wel longe ich habbe child ibeo. a werke and eke on dede.
þah ich beo of wynter old. to yong ich am on rede.
Vnned lif ich habbe ilad. and yet me þinkþ ich lede.
Whenne ich me biþenche. ful sore ich me adrede.
Mest al þat ich habbe idon. is idelnesse and chilce.
Wel late ich habbe me biþouht. bute god do me mylce.
Veole idel word ich habbe ispeke. seoþþe ich speke cuþe.
And feole yonge deden ido. þat me ofþincheþ nuþe.
Al to lome ich habbe agult. on werke and on worde.
Al to muchel ich habbe ispend. to lutel ileyd an horde.
Mest al þat me likede er. nv hit me mys lykeþ.
þe muchel folewaþ his wil. him seolue he biswikeþ.
Mon let þi fol lust ouer go. and eft hit þe likeþ.
Ich myhte habbe bet ido. hevede ich eny selhþe.
Nv ich wolde and i ne may. for elde. ne for vnhelþe.
Elde is me bistolen on. er þan ich hit wiste.
Ne may ich biseo me bifore. for smoke ne for myste.
Erwe we beoþ to donne god. vuel al to þriste.
More eye stondeþ mon of mon. þan him to cryste.
þe wel ne doþ hwile he may. hit schal him sore reowe.
hwenne alle men repen schule. þat heo ear seowe.
Dod to gode þat ye muwen. þe hwile ye beoþ alyue.
Ne lipne no mon to muchel. to childe ne to wyue.
þe him seolue for yet. for wiue oþer for childe.
he schal cumen on vuele stude. bute god him beo milde.
Sende vch sum god bivoren him. þe hwile he may to heouene.
Betere is on almes bivoren. þane beoþ after seouene.
Ne beo þe leouere þan þi seolf. þi mey ne þi mowe.
Sot is þat is oþer mannes freond. more þan his owe.
Ne lipne no wif to hire were. ne were to his wyue.
Beo vor him seolue vych mon. þe hwile he beoþ alyue.
Wis is þat him seolue biþenkþ. þe hwile he mot libbe.

Fig. 33 *A Moral Ode,* about 1250,
Oxford: Jesus College MS 1 Arch. 1. 29.

15350). Next we will examine a series of purely literary hands of the twelfth century, a period which was prolific in the production of calligraphic specimens – the period of large volumes, of fine bold ornamentation, and of a noble character of handwriting. A beautiful manuscript (Fig. 26) containing the commentary of Bede on Ezra was written for the Abbey of Cirencester between the years 1147 and 1176 – say about the middle of the century – and gives us a favourable impression of the work of a scriptorium in the West of England at that time (MS 3 Royal A. xii). Returning to Winchester, we have a splendid specimen of a Latin Bible written in the reign of Henry II – in double columns – and still preserved at Winchester. And again, travelling to the further west, we find coming from the monastery of St Mary of Buildwas, in Shropshire, a manuscript written with wonderful accuracy and finish (Fig. 29), Leviticus, with commentary, of the year 1176 (MS Harley 3038). Next we turn eastward and select a beautiful specimen of clear roundhand writing from a breviary of St Albans (that great school of English handwriting), of the middle of the century (MS Royal 2 A. x.). And from St Mary's of Reading, written about the year 1178, we have a fine manuscript of the *Diadema Monachorum* of Smaragdus (MS Royal 8 E. xviii.).

But a change was approaching when the beautiful curves of the twelfth century were to fall into the straight strokes and more serried ranks of the writing of the thirteenth century. This transition we may illustrate by a MS of the *Historia Scholastica* of Peter Comestor, dated in the year 1191–92 (Fig. 30) where the writing is rather of the smaller character of the later century. The full development of this later time is known to us by the hundreds of minutely-written manuscripts which have survived, and particularly by the numerous examples of the Bible which were produced in

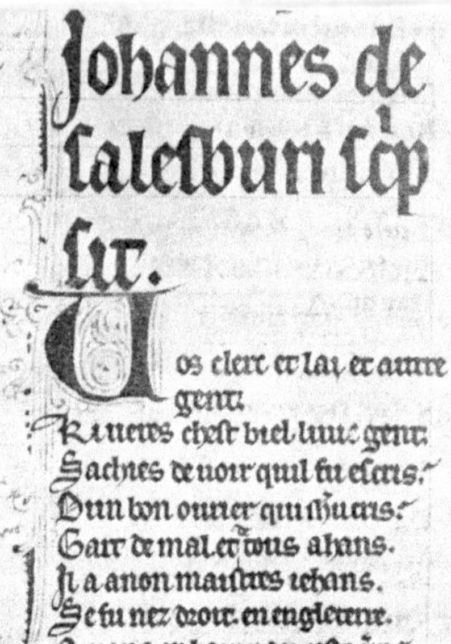

Fig. 34 John of Salisbury's *Lectionary*, AD 1269, British Library, MS Egerton 2569.

such quantities in the thirteenth century. As an instance of the latter we may take a manuscript written in the year 1254 (Fig. 31); and again a still finer specimen, also among the Royal manuscripts (1 D. i), undated, but written by a scribe calling himself William of Devon. It is also interesting to study the ornamentation of MSS of the twelfth and thirteenth centuries, in which will be seen the affinity between the writing and the art of the two periods – the broad drawing of the twelfth century being in keeping with the bold writing of the same time, and the minuter and more serried writing of the thirteenth century being reflected in the contemporary style of ornament. To continue our series of specimens of literary hands, we select an example of a very favourite class of manuscripts in the twelfth and thirteenth century – a bestiary, *Liber de natura Bestiarum*, written in the first half of the thirteenth

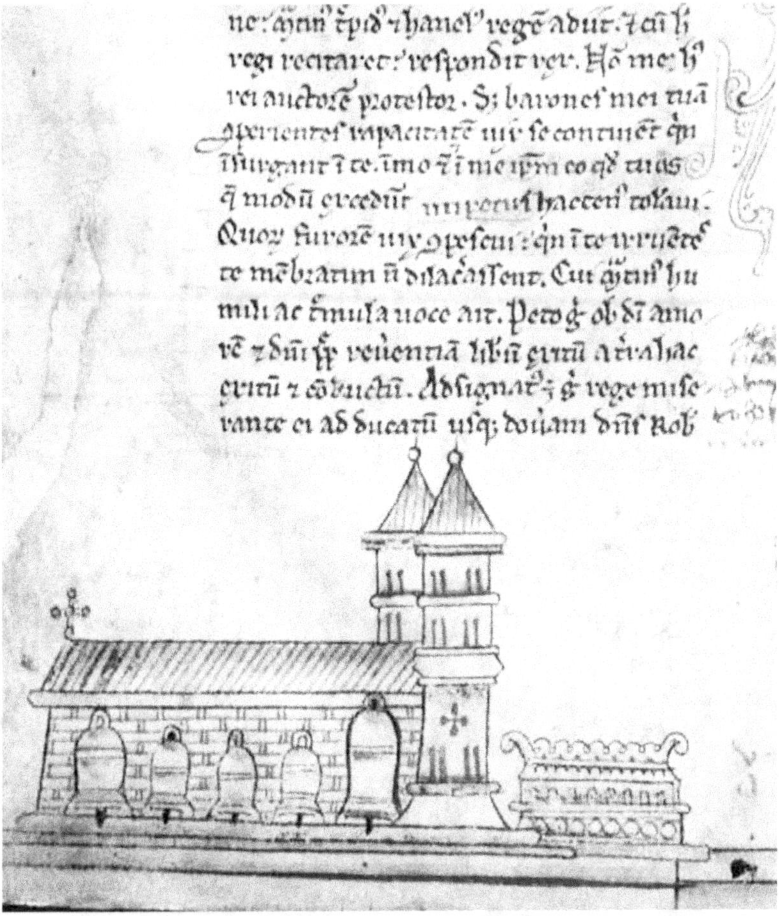

Fig. 35 Matthew Paris, *Historia Anglorum,* AD 1250–53, with picture of Westminster Abbey, British Library MS Royal 14 C. vii, f. 138 v.

century (MS Harley 3244); and, next, a fine specimen of handwriting, a Lectionary (Fig. 34) written at Mons in Hainault, for the doyenne of the monastery of Vaudru, by an English scribe, John of Salisbury, in 1269. In the time of Henry III, the most interesting figure in the monastery of St Albans is Matthew Paris,

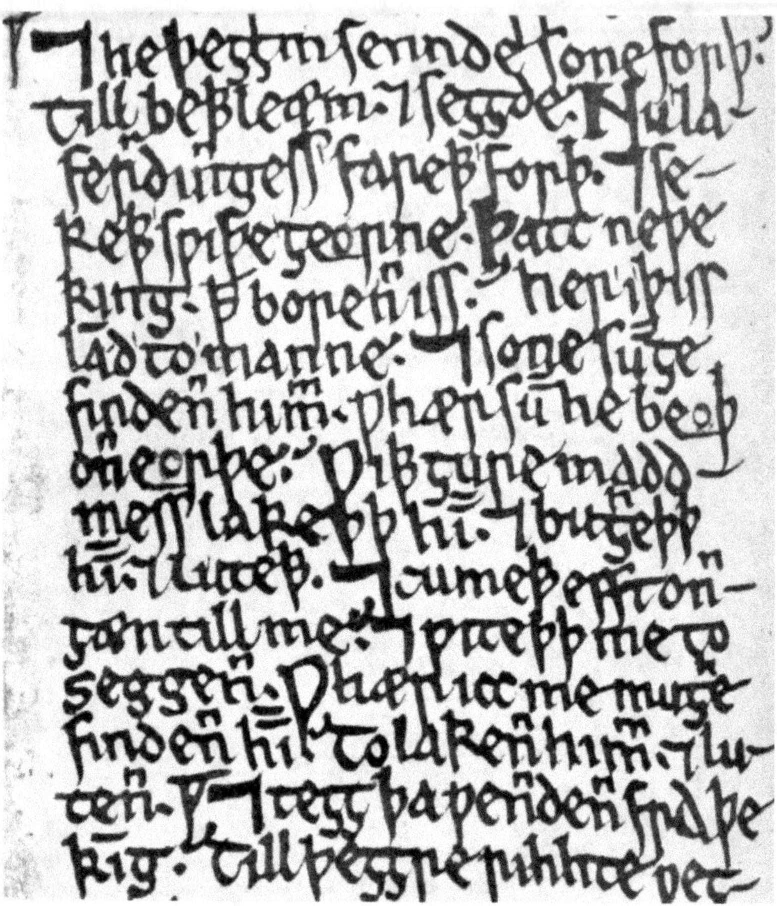

Fig. 36 *The Ormulum,* early thirteenth century, Oxford: Bodleian Library MS Junius 1.

the hiſtorian, a man of great learning and accomplishments. From his autograph *Hiſtoria Anglorum,* written in the years 1250-1253, we select a page as an example of a good working hand of the time and, as a specimen of outline drawing which may very probably be the work of Matthew Paris himself (Fig. 35).

Before leaving the thirteenth century, I will place before you three intereſting manuscripts written in the vernacular. Although

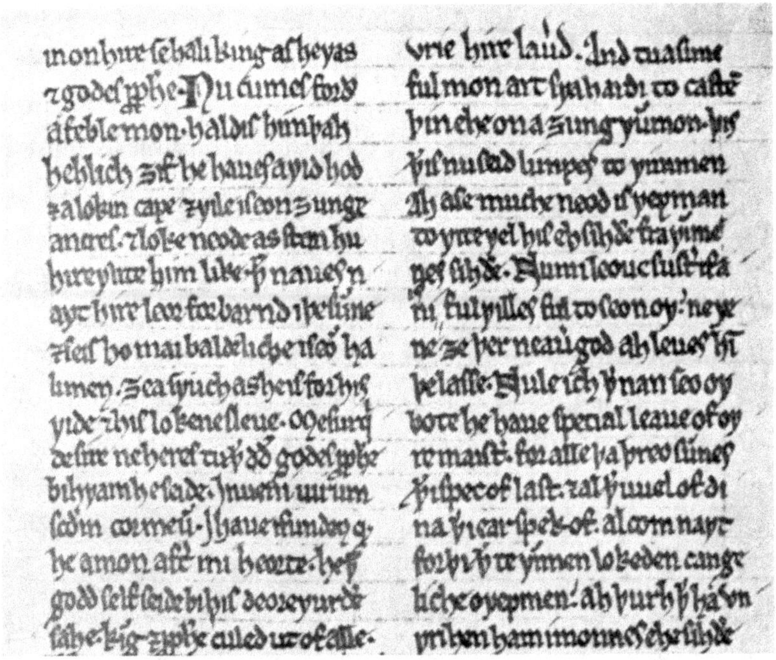

Fig. 37 *Ancren Riwle,* British Library MS Cotton Titus D. xviii.

after the Norman Conquest the Anglo-Saxon form of writing practically ceased to exist, yet certain English letters which were required for the expression of the English language remained in use – a survival which in a certain degree continued to give to a vernacular text a native aspect. One of the most famous English manuscripts of the early part of the thirteenth century is the *Ormulum* (at Oxford), being homilies on gospel lessons in metre by Orm or Ormin, written in the neighbourhood of Lincoln, in a rough powerful hand (Fig. 36). Another interesting manuscript is a copy of the *Ancren Riwle,* in English, a work composed for the nuns of Tarrant Kaines in Dorsetshire (Fig. 37). This manuscript is in the Midland dialect of the early part of the century – written in a good literary hand. A third document of general interest is a copy of the hymn which Handy Nicholas in Chaucer's *Miller's Tale* sang: 'And *Angelus ad Virginem* he sang.' This occurs in the MS Arundel 248 f. 154, in the British Library, with its musical setting and an English version written in the charter hand of the middle of the thirteenth century (Fig. 38).

The thirteenth century is the period of the climax of writing in Western Europe. From this date begins a deterioration, not very obvious at first, for we meet with many finely written manuscript of later date, but still a deterioration from the excellence of the earlier periods. The writing of the thirteenth century is exact and uniform and firm in its stroke; in the fourteenth century this stiffness is exchanged for a more flowing style and a more curving stroke. In the English literary hand of the fourteenth century, and more perceptibly in the latter half of the century, the influence of the cursive hand of the charters intrudes, and, combining with the more regular literary hand, helps to create a new style of writing for certain classes of literature. In fact, we have here only another instance of that law of development, whereby, after a particular form of literary writing has had a certain career, the cursive hand in vogue inevitably begins to intermingle and break down the integrity of the more formal hand. The cause is, of course, not far to seek: a book-hand is after all only an artificial production; while a cursive hand is the natural writing of its time.

Let us turn back for a moment to the origin of this cursive hand – the charter hand as we may conveniently call it. As above noted, the Norman conquerors brought with them their own official form of handwriting, in presence of which the native Anglo-Saxon hand was driven out of use. The continental cursive hands used in charters and other official documents, the diplomatic hands as

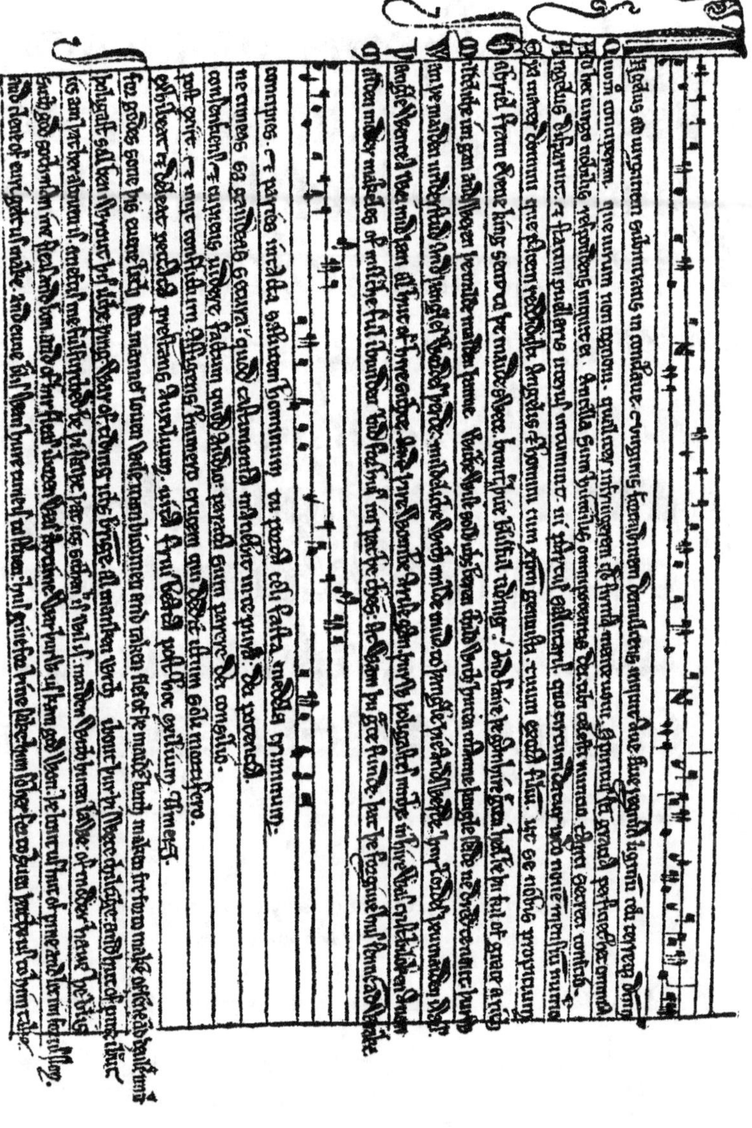

Fig. 38 *Angelus ad Virginem*, thirteenth century, British Library MS Arundel 248, f. 154.

Sire: volez vous graunter ⁊ gar
der ⁊ par vostre serment confer
mer au poeple dengletere les leys ⁊
les custumes a eux grauntees par
les aunciens roys dengletere voz
predecessours dreitureus ⁊ devotz
a dieu, ⁊ nomement les leys les
coustumes ⁊ les franchises graun
tees au clerge ⁊ au poeple par le
glorieus roy seint Edward vostre
predecessour.

Fig. 39 Coronation service, AD 1308,
British Library MS Harley 2901.

they have been called, were the lineal descendants of that Roman cursive hand which passed through so many vicissitudes among the foreign nations of Western Europe. When the great reform of the literary writing of the Frankish empire was brought about by the efforts of Charlemagne, the cursive official hand was not so much affected. More regularity certainly was introduced, but many of the characteristics of the earlier hand remained. The cursive hand, so to say, was not pruned down; but retained much of the fanciful growths and extravagances of the older time. Thus, the cursive official hand which was introduced by the Normans into England, while it had by that time conformed in a great measure to the exact pattern of the literary style, still retained those long strokes and flourishes which marked the exuberant hand of the Merovingian period. If you examine a series of official documents of the early reigns succeeding the Conquest, you will see how persistently the old tradition clings to the new English charter-hand, and how long a time passes before the long strokes get pruned away. Even to the last, right down to the end of the fifteenth century, they will be found occasionally surviving in the first line, sometimes too in the last line, of a document by way of ornamentation.

As time passes, the charter hand, of course, receives the characteristics of the successive periods, on the same lines as the literary hand, and when we arrive at the fourteenth century we find, as we have noticed in the case of the literary hand, that a flowing style and one of curving strokes succeeds the stiff regular hand of the previous century. It is at this epoch that the cursive hand begins prominently to affect the literary hand, to break down the tradition of exact formality, and gradually to merge into it, producing the hybrid style to which I have referred. Still, the formal literary style was generally maintained for such books as liturgies and sacred books in Latin, the texts of which had traditionally been always inscribed in a calligraphic form; and even down to the close of the fifteenth century this formality is observed. For general literature, however, the new, rounder hand, which could be written so much more expeditiously, became the favourite style; and no doubt the path for the common adoption of this hand had in some measure been prepared by the increasing production of manuscripts in the vernacular, for which it was more suitable.

A few specimens will illustrate these remarks. First we will look at a liturgical book – a psalter, written and ornamented in the eastern counties of the School of Norwich, about the first quarter of the fourteenth century (MS Arundel 83) – the writing being the formal book hand. And of the extreme end of the century we select a handsome Bible, written in the same character and ornamented in a most artistic manner (MS Royal 1 E. ix). Of manuscripts influenced by the charter-hand, our earliest example is drawn from a coronation service prepared for the coronation of Edward II in 1308 (MS Harley 2901). The page represented (Fig. 39) is the secular part of the service, the coronation oath, and is written, not in the formal book hand, but in one in which the forms of the charter hand largely predominate. Next, we have a vernacular manuscript, the *Remorse of Conscience* or the *Aȝenbite of Inwit* (Fig. 40), of the year 1340. And this is succeeded (Fig. 41) by a chronicle of English history written at St Albans (MS Harley 3634) about the year 1388 in the writing influenced by the charter-hand, which has here settled down into a thoroughly workmanlike style.

But while the extended production of popular literature no doubt tended to foster the use of the less formal character of writing of which we have been speaking, there was in some instances

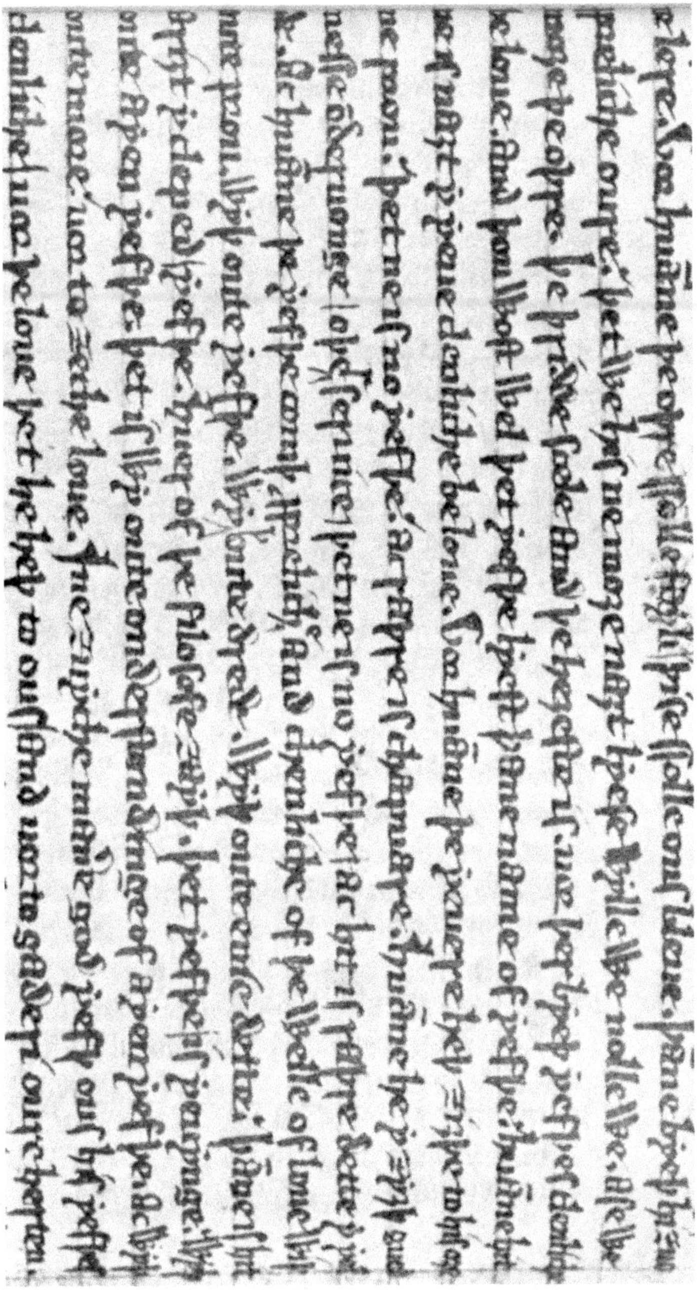

Fig. 40 *Azenbite of Inwit*, 1340, British Library MS Arundel 57.

Fig. 41 Chronicle, St Albans, c.1388, British Library MS Harley 3634.

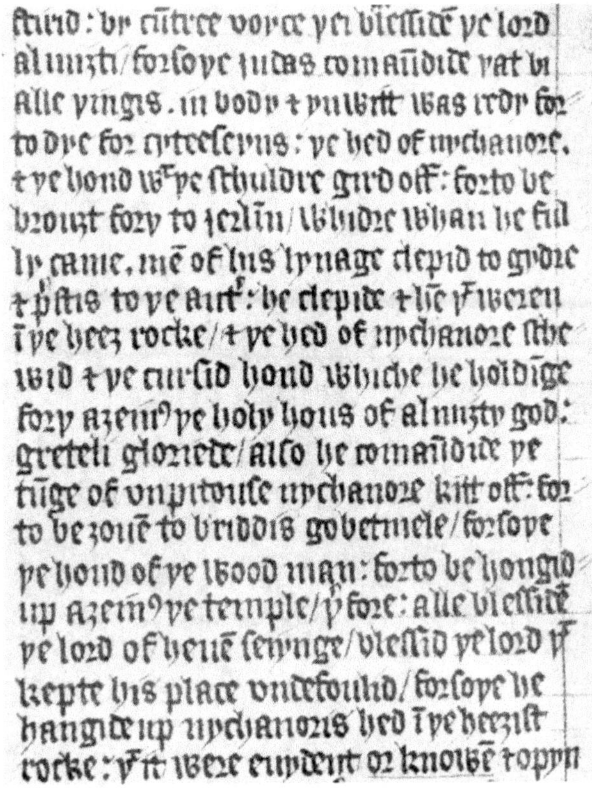

Fig. 42 Wycliffe's Bible, latter part of the fourteenth century, British Library MS Add 15580.

a kind of reaction. Certain works in English literature became so popular that the professional scribes found it worth their while to write them in a more careful style; or an author might have the copy of his work, intended for presentation to his patron, executed in a handsome way. Two carefully written manuscripts of Wycliffe's Bible will illustrate this. The first (Fig. 42), written in the latter part of the fourteenth, century, in a good firm hand; the other (Fig. 43) written for Thomas of Woodstock, Duke of Gloucester, who was put to death in 1397.

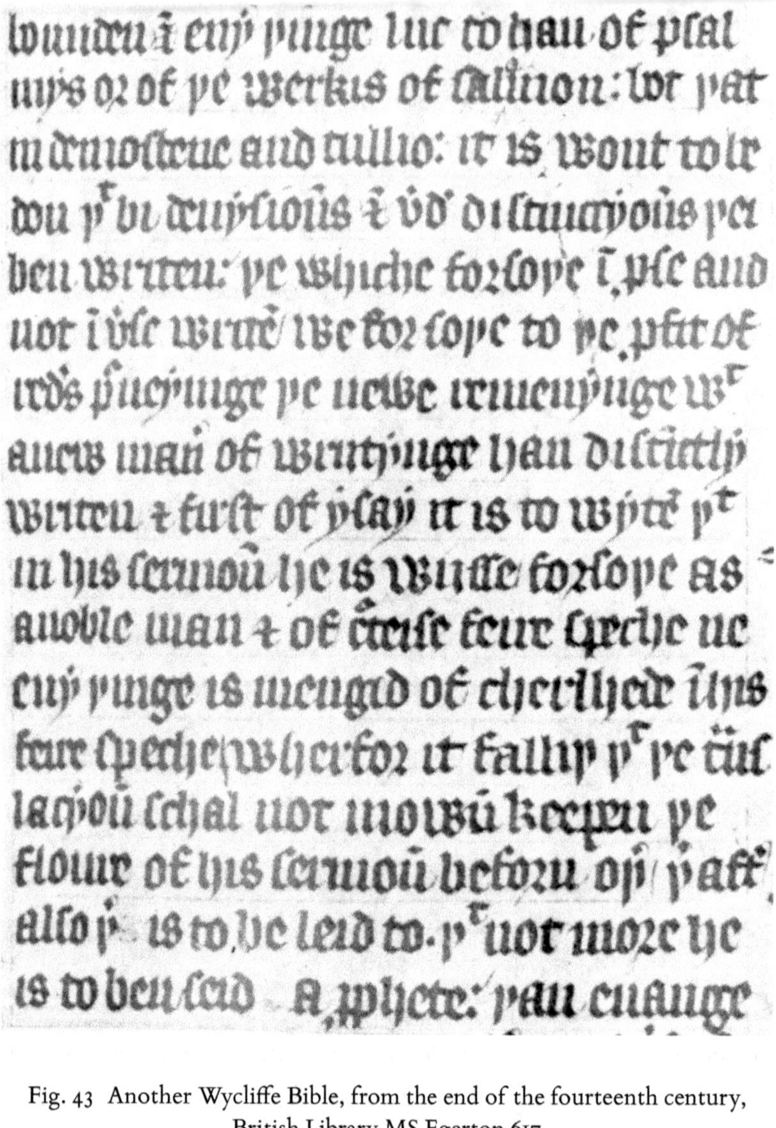

Fig. 43 Another Wycliffe Bible, from the end of the fourteenth century, British Library MS Egerton 617

Fig. 44 *Robert of Gloucester's Chronicle,* fourteenth century, Cambridge: Trinity College MS R. 4. 26.

Tauerners vntil hem · trewely tolden þe same
Whit wyn of Oseye · and reed wyn of Gascoigne
Of þe Ryn and of þe Rochel · þe roost to defie

Passus primus de visione

What þis mountaigne bymeneþ · and þe merke dale
And þe feld ful of folk · I shal yow faire shewe

A louely lady of leere · in lynnen yclothed
Cam doun from a castel · and called me faire
And seide sone slepestow · seestow þis peple
How bisie þei ben · alle aboute þe maze
The mooste partie of þis peple · þat passeþ on þis erþe
Haue þei worship in þis world · þei wilne no bettre
Of ooþ heuene þan here · holde þei no tale

I was afered of hire face · þeiȝ she faire weere
And seide mercy madame · what is þis to meene

The tour on þe toft quod she · truþe is þerInne
And wolde þt ye wrouȝte · as his word techeþ
ffor he is fader of feiþ · and formed yow alle
Boþe wt fel and wt face · and yaf yow fyue wittes
ffor to worshipe hym þerwiþ · while þt ye ben here
And þerfore he hiȝte þe erþe · to helpe yow echone

Fig. 45 *Piers Plowman,* last third of fourteenth century, Cambridge: Trinity College MS B. 15.17, fol. 5r.

Fig. 46 Harley Chaucer, about 1400, British Library MS Harley 7334.

Laſtly, I will cross the border and present to you two intereſting English MSS written early in the fifteenth century. The firſt is the Harley Chaucer (Fig. 46); the other (Fig. 47) is a manuscript of Hoccleve, written for presentation to Henry Prince of Wales, afterwards Henry V (MS Harley 4866), in the ſtyle blending the charter and literary hands, but here moulded into a set and calligraphic form. The manuscript is of course well-known on account of the portrait of Chaucer which it contains. We can see sufficient

ffor it is vnto verray pees a foo
Whan men in a purpos maliciouse
Acorden þat pees is to god greuous
Which pees was twixe herodes & pilat
And in which maner pees is wers þanne debat

A feyned pees eeke is to pees contrary
Also and which was þe pees of Iudas
kissyng crist lord whom þat þis day
Any which pees vsed is or þat was
ȝe god forbede me by seynt thomas
The kus of Iudas is now wyde sprad
Tokenes of pees ben but smal loue is had

Men countrefete in wordis tullius
And folwe in werk Iudas or genylon
Many in hony worde and many a kus
Ther is but venym on þe conclusion
And þe pyne galle all turnyth vp so doun
Ther serueth naght of pees but contenance
ffor al þe peyntyd chere and daliance

Fig. 47 Hoccleve, early fifteenth century
British Library MS Harley 4866..

affinity between this writing and the type in which Caxton put forth his early books (Fig. 48) to appreciate the fact that the new printing type (though of Low Countries origin) would not have had an altogether unfamiliar aspect to the Englishman who was accustomed to read the English MSS of the period.

First shal ye clepe to your counceyll a felwe of your frendes
that ben specyall / For Salamon saith / Many a frende haue
thou / But among a thousand chese the one to be thy coun-
ceyllour / For al be hit so that thou first telle thy counceyll
to felwe / thou maist after telle thy counceyll to mo folke yf
hit be nede / But loke alway that thy councellours haue tho
thre condicions that I haue said beforn / that is to saye that
they be trewe. wise. and of old experience / And werke not
allewey in every nede by one councellour allone / For som
tyme hit behoueth to be counceylled by many / For Salamon saith / Saluation of thinges is there where be many
counceyllours / Now sith I haue told yow. of whiche folke
that ye shold be councelled / Now will I telle whiche coun
ceyll ye shal eschewe. First ye shal eschewe the councellyng
of foles / For Salamon saith take no counceyll of a fool.

Fig 48 Caxton's printing type (type 2) in
The Dictes and Sayengis of the Philosophres, 1477.

Little can or need be said for the progress of literary handwriting in England in the fifteenth century. It was a period of decadence. The round handwriting of the fourteenth century gradually grows stiff and angular – not with the accurate stiffness of the thirteenth century, but with that of careless, ill-formed writing. It was only, as already observed, in liturgical or sacred books, as a rule, that the old formality of the literary hand was maintained; and this latter hand we see adopted for the type of the early printed English liturgies.

Sources of Illustrations

Thompson's Original Edition
Figures 3, 5a, 6, 7, 8, 10, 13, 15, 18, 20, 24, 26, 29, 31, 38, 39, 41, 47

Walter William Skeat
Twelve Facsimiles of Old English Manuscripts
Clarendon Press, 1892
Figures 1, 27, 33

Walter Wilson Greg
Facsimiles of Twelve Early Manuscripts in the Library of Trinity College Cambridge
Oxford University Press, 1913
Figures 21, 23, 28, 45

Daniel Berkeley Updike
Printing Types: Their History, Forms and Use
Harvard University Press, 1922
Figure 48

Edward Maunde Thompson
Introduction to Greek and Latin Palaeography
Clarendon Press, 1912
Figures 2, 4, 5b, 9, 11, 12, 14, 15, 16, 19, 22, 25, 30, 32, 34, 36, 37, 40, 42, 43, 44, 46

The British Library
Figure 35 & front cover

Index

INDEX

INDEX

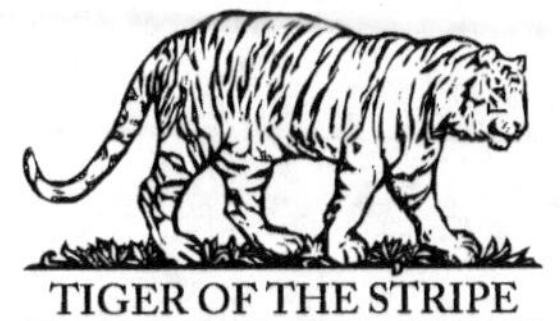

Typeset in the United Kingdom
in Monotype Bembo Book Pro
by Tiger of the Stripe

www.ingramcontent.com/pod-product-compliance
Lightning Source LLC
LaVergne TN
LVHW020052110826
845155LV00021B/70

* 9 7 8 1 9 0 4 7 9 9 1 0 8 *